AF580663

Remnants of Change

REMNANTS

of CHANGE

Poems Inspired by the Lithographs of

ANCEL·E·NUNN

by Samuel C. Woolvin

Library of Congress Catalog Card Number 91-090965

International Standard Book Number 0-9627096-1-1

Design and production by Whitehead & Whitehead

To our wives, Alma and Reneta

Some always stood, above the winter fires
When prairies crackled, flame and shifting soot
Demanded change of matted stems of grass,
Blazes lapping at those knotted roots.
Spared by chance its twisted limbs evolved
To shade this pleasant knoll whose site would grow,
Soon outlined by a pathway to the well,
Where fieldstone rimmed its cool gift far below.

Here is that tethered astrolabe, creaking pulley
Tugged by children sloshing their burdens
From well to porch, stave buckets mossy with time
When jostling cycles were wet reminders
That each hollow splash was an invocation, a prayer
Answered for those who dared to live
Beside the cooling zephyrs in the tree,
Holding that deep cylinder in reverence,
Knowing that so long as water remained
It would be a mirror, a tiny distant mirror.
Reflecting skittering clouds,
Reflecting in turn, tiny distant faces
Smiling down into its cool depths.

Where are those footsteps now, lost in time?
Each return to the cabin built strength
Into limbs that would leave forever
The place of being. And the fieldstones?
Relics they are, each crumbled back to soil,
The leaves? They were whisked away,
And even the old titan of an oak felt its autumn,
Tiring of its vigil it slumped to one side,
Losing its majesty in a tangle of fractured branches
Whose gift was that of returning in its cycle,
Its dignity towered above the prairie, until the end,
Before and after the voices of children.

Foreword

By Billy Porterfield

> *There is, one knows not what sweet mystery about this sea, whose gentle awful stirrings seem to speak of some hidden soul beneath . . .*
>
> —Ishmael, in Herman Melville's *Moby-Dick*

THESE POEMS are the work of a weathered seeker—an aging Ishmael, if you like—a landlocked sailor of fortune who has found himself shipwrecked, but blessedly afloat, upon a wide-rolling prairie-sea of drought-drowned dreams and dreamlike reveries.

A wooden box coughed up from the bowels of the doomed vessel bobs to the surface, and Samuel Woolvin clings to it as though it were a lifeboat. It serves as that, and more. Sam discovers it contains the log of the ship's epic journey as recorded by his captain, one Ahab named Ancel.

In this, my Melvillean version of the ups and downs and ultimate destruction of the *Texas Pequod,* Ishmael finds not only Ahab's diary but Ahab himself yet alive. They team to complete the log, their muses re-embarking upon the great, diuturnal journey to resurrect and trace the images—which do their best to hide, like the ghosts they are—upon the vast dreamscape of Texas.

In a literal, day-world sense, the journalist in me requires that I tell you that Sam Woolvin is a medical doctor in Corpus Christi and a longtime friend of artist Ancel Nunn, who lives and works in his Morning Town Studio outside Palestine in the pines of Anderson County. A collector of Nunn's work, Woolvin has for years and rather secretly, out of modesty, been writing poems inspired by the paintings and drawings of his friend. One day Woolvin was one of 110 patrons to receive from Nunn a priceless limited edition of scenes Ancel had sketched of a vanishing Texas. Sam lifted the sketchbook, *Remnants of Change,* from its wooden case and opened its leather-bound cover to find, on archival paper, forty lithographs of the rural Texas that many of us as youths saw passing before our uncomprehending eyes. The evocation, like other Ancel summonings, moved Sam to poetry, and this that you have before you is the result.

In the fall of 1982, in a letter to Ancel, Sam spoke of the effect on him of a painting by Nunn called *The New Road.* He wrote that it "strikes such a chord in my imagination it is difficult to express what I feel about that picture. When I look at it I undergo a mental transport or emotional metamorphosis into some other world. It is a place that I once thought I would want to be, but which I never was, only in flights of fancy, yet it is commonplace enough. But you have designed what it means in that one work. You are as literary a person as you are an artist, because you can compress a welter of words and word images into art that initiates a tumble of ideas from the beholder. No two people could share the identical feeling, but the quixotic timelessness and emotional associations with your works are now becoming part of our heritage. You have taught me much, and I am grateful."

Nunn's reputation is secure as anything in this temporal place. Most of us know of his long and tireless sojourn to draw and paint man and the world about him out of the corner of time we so nihilistically inhabit. For all the detailed and seemingly realistic precision which makes his rural pictures instantly recognizable, Ancel has never been satisfied with leaving a record of surfaces. He knows well Thomas Carlyle's admonition: "All visible things are emblems; what thou seest is not there on its own account; strictly taken, is not there at all: Matter exists only spiritually, and to represent some Idea, and body it forth."

The first implication of every pencil, litho crayon or brush stroke that Ancel Nunn puts to paper or cloth must contain the prophecy of the last. "The sum must be in the beginning as well as in the end," he said to me once. We were sitting in his studio, he before a canvas, folded into half a man who still dwarfed me. No artist, save perhaps Gutzon Borglum, is as big and powerful as Ancel in physique and temperament. Odd that Ancel's medium and style is so tedious and specific in its execution. It would take him forever to paint Mt. Rushmore. It is this contradiction in Ancel Nunn, this war and rapture between the roughhewn and the polished, the workman and the artist, the provider and improvident, that has so fascinated those who know him.

That day, Ancel was serious as a god and talking like one. Or Carlyle. I thought it astonishing, and wonderful, that a man who had spent his body and soul evoking images, painting the visible, could turn to me in all candor and say that the gods are invisible even in their display, and their nature unknowable.

A pondering heart looks deep into Nunn's work and realizes that his plainest weathered boards and broken glass and dry grass seem haunted, not by an illustrator's easy sentimentality, but by something strange and almost numinous in the remoteness with which it possesses familiar places. It is something felt rather than seen, as if Ancel does indeed paint the unseen, that which lurks in the ruins of our ambition. Certainly this is what Sam saw that spawned these poems. Sam sees the unseen too, only he embodies it as them, calling them nymphs and naiads, nimbi, omens and nomads.

In the shadow of drawings they linger,

he writes,

Faint whispers—faint remnants of sounds.

But then Woolvin can't resist echoing Ancel, for they are soulmates, when he observes,

Man will chant to all manner of forces,
Knowing little or nothing of the truth.

The old prairie, like the Mariner's ancient sea, is their purview, their homecoming of reality and dream. It proves fathomable, unfathomable. Drawn to it, repelled by it (the whispering wraiths are like Elijahs warning them away from the Pequods, the wreckages of the prairie), they heave to like Ahab and Ishmael, ready to sound its depths.

For his part, Woolvin launches into descriptive poems for each of Ancel's forty sketches—reprinted here from *Remnants of Change*—as they move across the abandoned landscape from well, windlass and water bucket to house, barn, ruin after ruin which is the tale of the American Outback. Now and then there is life: a boy in a barber's chair, remnants of a pasture baseball game, the circus come to town, a woman milking a cow. Forty or one, this is an impassioned epic poem, the greatest I've read on the Texas saga. Sam is a Homer of wide horizons, a medical doctor who waits until now, late in life, to put down his microscope and raise his majestic voice in unison with his old friend, the artist.

Sam's cadence and reach is biblical, recalling Tyndale's *Pentateuch,* which shook the boy Shakespeare and loosed his tongue. But between the Elizabethan and the 20th Century American Woolvin looms the leviathan Melville, yet a melancholy stowaway from 19th Century New Bedford. You will see that Sam Woolvin is deep as any whaledive, and the comparison to Melville is apt. Not the spinner of South Sea romances, but the Melville who died a stoic if obscure poet, so Moby-Dick dark that the *New York Times,* upon his death in 1891, blacked out on his first name and dubbed him Henry instead of Herman.

In the generations since, we have made the mysterious Melville one of our fathers who fits the passion of the moment, and it seems I'm doing it here. But the self-taught, deep sounding Melville has always beckoned—like the harpooner Tashtego waving his dead, red arm from the back of the whale—from behind the seaweed beard of our prairie painter Ancel Nunn. Nunn has Melville's depth-charged soul. With his brush he stirs up the lees of things. And he requires the sea-room of Texas to tell the Truth in. It comes as no surprise that in this outing, so consecrated with the salt of the inscrutableness of the created, imaged world, Ancel would bring along as his mate/poet the Ishmael/Sam. Looking into Sam's eyes, you see a man uncommonly conscientious for a seaman, endued with a deep natural reverence, full with outward portent and inward presentiment. And he will not cross Ancel. They are one. In this voyage, Sam is a mighty Melville, tongue afire in the Heaven and Hell of Texas.

Like Melville in the poem, *Clarel,* Woolvin eases the bite of irony that aches here and there, suggesting *Loomings* might have been a satiric epic. Instead, he adopts a high and clear-eyed elegiac tone, proper to the backward gaze of the sketches. It is an elegy in mood, not always in form. The constraints of Homeric hexameter and pentameter can't hold him, although he uses it. Sam begins in free verse, shifts to rhyme, and, having set a New World pattern of variation, moves in a Melvillean vortex that swims and swallows up couplets heroic and closed, blank verse Miltonesque, free verse Whitmanesque, sonnets Shakespearean and stanzas Spenserian, or almost. I am reminded of Whitman's remark in his *An American Primer* that the English language, as employed by Americans, is grandly lawless like the race who use it, that we break out of the little laws to make higher ones. Woolvin has done that here. He uses fierce, limber, lasting words, and shows a consummate individuality in the way he employs meter and accent.

His is an incantation at times, celebratory before grand vistas:

I glory in space encompassed by unyielding winds,
Cerulean limits yet boundless in turbulent motion,
Of seeing the infinite stretch of soil where I tread,
Deprived of restraints that cease in the depths of an ocean.

And he is certainly malty as old Walty when he pauses to watch Ancel's marvelous homesteader douse himself pump-side on a warm summer's night:

His sigh of relief is audible,
The handle had creaked, the bar rattled,
A coyote is yipping in the draw below.
A warm popping tin roof complains less now,
He savors the ancient ceremony of ablution,
He is alone, with his creator.

Here, pausing in the atonement of purgation, Nunn and Woolvin baptize humankind as well as the old nester and themselves, even as they pass on down the road to sift through the relics of his and his neighbor's—and their own—rise and fall on the spent prairie.

At Fort Phantom Hill, where Ancel sketches the last-standing stone chimneys of the encampment, Woolvin summons ghostly dragoons:

They pass the artist's gaze in double file,
Hiyo, hiyo, the petards droop on poles
Hot-clutched to sway in rhythmic canter step,
So brief their time, Fort Phantom Hill's patrols.

They come upon a powder magazine, which Sam describes as

a mausoleum attuned to death / Its thundersticks and powder
/ Kept a'waiting for some spark / To set free its hoary voice, . . .

Across the land they sense a *timed but timeless cycle of night to silvered day.* Male sanctuaries are *kiva quiet,* kitchens are cold and lifeless, the school houses closed. And while Ancel draws them thusly, Sam must ask of rural Texans:

Where are their gardens, ballrooms, schools,
Their quiet verandas, evensong, and teas?
Those are their dreams, their wonderment at us,
They are the ships, and we, the restless seas.

All has collapsed for them, as it will for us in the cities, and the great shroud of the prairie rolls on as it rolled five thousand years ago. Like Job and Ishmael, Ancel and Sam are escaped to tell thee. And we see that the wooden box that contained Ancel's sketchbook became their life raft, and we are buoyed up by this wondrously engraved time capsule and its attendant poems, floating for our day and night on a soft and dirge-like main.

Welcome to our life-buoy. The drama's begun anew.

Remnants of Change

Warm Summer's Night

The artist, knowing his roots
Covers our memories with a black dome,
This is the abysmal sphere of silence,
A place broken by intruding sounds,
Some familiar, some only perceived,
Seeping through night's curtain
Throughout the quietude of space
Where errant breezes tantalize scorched soil,
This parched domain awaits always for water,
It is the transient sustenance of existence,
It pours across the lithograph,
It streams down about the pump,
His sigh of relief is audible,
The handle had creaked, the bar rattled,
A coyote is yipping in the draw below,
A warm popping tin roof complains less now,
He savors the ancient ceremony of ablution,
He is alone, with his creator.

Little does he think of gaseous matter
Clustering and swirling in space,
The ebb and flow of galaxies is beyond
The reach of one who dimly gazes at infinity,
Perhaps, only perhaps he recollects polaris
This dot about which all seems
To rotate in the gentle arcs of constellations,
He may sense, that in eons to come,
In new epochs where parsecs measure,
Long after the pump has crumbled,
Those steady patterns of spin
Will bring new terrestrials to the fore,
Some new pole star will emerge, to gleam,
Alone, alone in the fastness of the cosmos.

Tonight he will muse on the caress of water,
The whimsey of nature, the bawling of a cow,
His union with a puzzling, hostile universe,
The prices at auction, waxing his boots,
An earache, or a broken cylinder—essentials;
These considerations are now made kinder
And more energizing by the presence
Of that pail, on a warm summer's night.

Dwelling of Naiads

When did it first breach the soil?
First, a gentle trickle of moisture,
Hidden there in the red loamy hillock,
Gradually welling up to the surface,
A torrent of the microcosm of loam,
Here were Spring's droplets swelling leaves,
Winter's moisture mottling twigs,
Summer's promise and Autumn's freshet,
Here was the source, the nidus of rivers
Yet to be, not yet conceived from earth,
Pulled down along its rivulets
In the embrace of gravity,
Down, down, lower, on the gentle slope.

Forest murmurs sang its lullaby,
Across the virgin landscape stillness was
Immersed in its green coverlet, the pine,
Gum, holly, dogwood—each season rolled back
Until land, stripped of its color lay exposed,
Its mantle bare as broomtwigs clawed
In frantic motion the wintry skies,
A place where ice glaze formed on puddles,
Now a dwelling of Naiads.

A continuing host of visitants
Watched the morns and twilights,
Moving on where woody fragments lay,
Pushed about by some scratching thing,
Sniffing the moss, lapping cool water
Now deeply running from its active spring.
Each generation prowled for tiny eternities
These woodlands, sensing the guardian presence
Of ancient Naiads, creatures of the source,
Brides of the forested glade
Where conifers graced the sunlit naves
Soaring high above sonorous pipes
Once held by satyrs in their caprine hands.

Dare we seek some visionary? What nymphs
Stared down into that sacred pool?
When did aegis-bearing Zeus
Toss his crashing bolts into some copse
Of trees, burning away old growth?
How many fled the silvery descent
Of the falcon in its gyre?
Who shared that hundred thousand years
Of Olympian legends ensconced in the water
Trickling ever downward, to the valley edge,
The gift of the Naiads?

In time they came; the Dryads,
Painted wanderers pressing chert
Whose flakes sank into its rim,
Now the forest held an acrid smoke
Curling up from middens,
Here scraped hides were dried,
Here some fatigued Angelina
Ground seeds, turning her stone
To be left with others along the rim
Of the pool, forming yet another enclosure,
Deepening with each passing generation,
Forming its crystalline font.

They fell in ambush, toiled, grew old,
Looked sideways at the dappled reflections,
Saw the changing rays of moonsilver,
Smiled at the flickering patterns of light
From campfires; their stories were told,
Oral and memorized, their legacies
Were alive with symbolism and song,
Their history was strewn as pebbles
Or bones, or scrapers, along the rim,
They endured in a primal posture,
Quietly reflecting on the dwelling place,
Its gift gurgled upward from unseen strata,
Here on a summer's eve Hasinai flutes
Would evoke somber moodswings of a people,
Here the serious path of a people bending
In their symbiosis with nature endured,
Theirs were Pan's pipes summoning the Naiads.

They came, the strange hairy ones,
Pushing on to Anahuac, heavy with beads,
Metallic tools, and great pot lids;
Strangers to all, they persisted, the tree eaters,
Tearing at the forest was an obsession,
They slashed at spirit trees, great giants
There from the beginning,
Broad steel blades changed forever
Familiar trails and old landmarks,
But it was disease the Caddo feared,
Decimated clans bore father and son
To common graves; drove the women
Into pockets of final despair.
Where Naiads sang there arose contagion,
The gods had decreed death whose hands
Clutched at the survivors,
Death rode into the forest as surely
As the pool fell into darkness,
Shadowed by the winds of conflict.

The old ones faded into darkness
Enveloped by fear in a spirit world,
Their prayers were unattended in
This chasm cursed with change.
Those whose counsel passed with pipes
Looked on in helpless wonderment.
Bypassed in this inflamed torment
Wrenching those doomed to fade.
Soon the last moccasined footfall
Passed the dark pool, still flowing
Among the red oaks and hickory.
Just above, on the rise,
Displacing flicker and wren
Notched rows of shaved logs
Metamorphosed; a tin sheathed steeple
Thrust upward, as do all sabers
Held high above their fallen adversaries,
It gleamed in sunlight,
Where once a leafy canopy
Roofed the tiny pool.

Naiads heard new sounds,
Strange music resonated,
The reedy timbre of a wheezing organ
Lifted those new voices
Whose refinement of old themes
Sung through time in other forests,
Across waters unknown to Angelina
Were the voices and music of the land.
Where once was chipping and fitting
Of flint, new stones appeared,
They lay about the shallow basin,
Now dressed and mortised
They encased a pool where flitting bugs
Were pelted by raindrops.
Here the pale waters found one aperture
Recessed for the outpouring
Of lifegiving waters that ran down
Into the valley below, forever changed
As was the dwelling of Naiads.

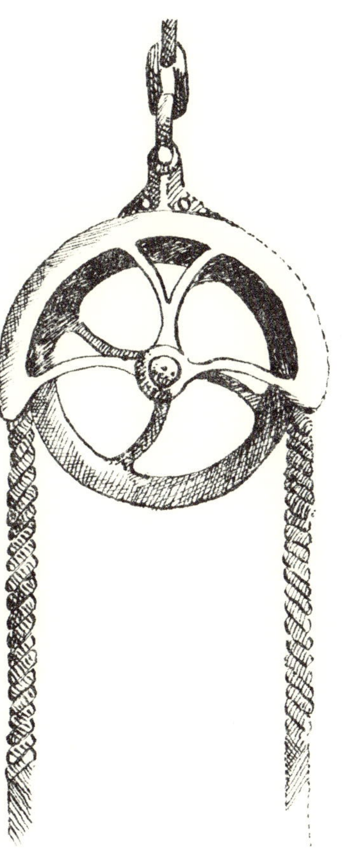

The Alpha and Omega

Sullen and friendless, beyond dull despair,
In brooding starkness, strippèd of hope,
Uniquely each beginning was a prayer,
A homesite stage for man to cope,
With any quest a newness bore its price,
Such overburdens, step by painful stride,
Pressed out the memory of some kinder place
Here blew the wind, and remnants of their pride.

Their chance enclosures wrested from this soil
Had seen so many camps o'errun or burned,
Muted murmurs sank into these hills
Replaced by new pyres, purged, then overturned.
Blocking passage lay those mounted tribes
Who ventured out into this fragile sphere,
Touching victim with rattling feathered coup,
To leave their fallen stretched upon a bier.

Sharp outcroppings shed their layered stone
To be aligned in courses, dressed, and squared,
Defining home, remuda, well, and pen,
A netlike domicile where life was snared,
Entrapped within the dreams bound by that space
From undulating valley, draw, or hill
Stretched all about the fiery blaze above,
The maw of summer, or the arctic chill.

Ranges savaged through the endless pleistocene
Revealed omegas when extinction reigned,
Each species destined from its gloried past
Would trumpet victory, or join the slain.
Flint knappers left darts among bleached ribs,
Their life suspended on thin, hafted points,
This prairie baptistry where names were called
For unction that old gods anoint.

What poultice soothed the crouping, fevered babe?
When were the rites of manhood brought before
Weary parents gathered by some fire?
When did their hopes pass through a splintered door?
How fared the cattle at the blizzard's end?
What prayers relieved the desiccating drought?
What burdens etched their wrinkled weathered skin?
When perished childhood thoughts with aging doubt?

Each season has merged with its fellows
Past homesteads where most sought their lot,
Dim forces that bound them together,
Were the powers unravelling their knot.
Peer at this roughness—what haven?
Hear echoes when space scarce has bounds,
In the shadow of drawings they linger,
Faint whispers—faint remnants of sounds.
Black vultures still circle hot currents
That rise from the shimmer of soil
Stained bloody by ages of hunting,
Then scratched by the ethics of toil.

At the end, Omega triumphant
As horsemen whose rumble is death
Came, blades glinting, raised up at noonday,
To cut down the dawn's shibboleth.

So sacred one's home, yet so fleeting,
Their prologue was past, deeds were done,
Stone epitaphs lie as recorded
For those—oblivion, oblivion.

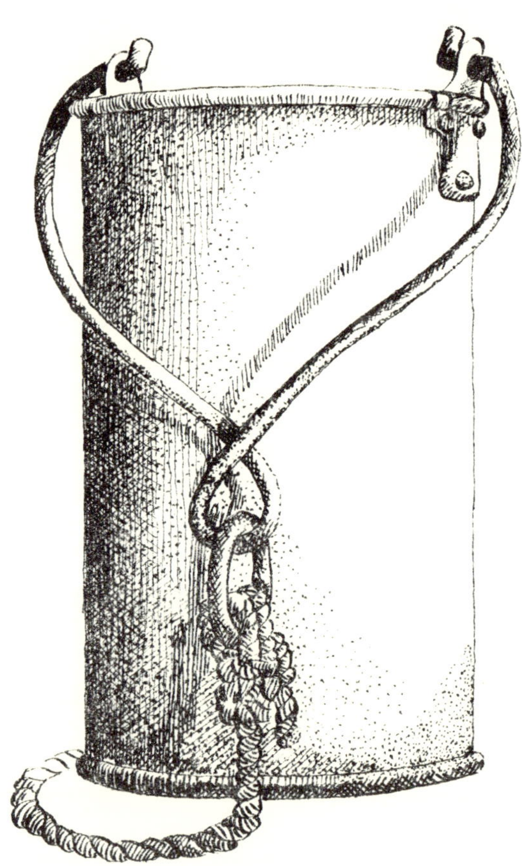

The Gathering of Waters

Our world crust
Is a changing sponge,
Where seepage above
Runs in watery flow
To charge those aquifers
Of common existence
In the blessings of water.
Far from magmatic lava
In that fuming iron core
Far, far below the rotar.

Thirsty stems and shoots
Parched to crispness
Survive for that hour
When a peppery line
Of summer raindrops
Bears down upon his spread,
A bleached wasteland.

Through dusty lids,
Scarce blinking eyes
Ponder the rare imagery
Of visions oft lifting up
A thousand invocations
To whatever personal deity
Presides over this expanse,
This theater of the round,
A gathering of waters.

This is a confluence of emotions,
A tributary of extreme hope,
It is tied to God's arid universe,
Water hoisted, clinking up
In short spurts from its bore,
With piston squeals of agony,
In cries of complaining gears,
Sending forth mandalas,
Metallic chants of desperation,
Where the blessed turbulence
Borne on fitful, spiteful breezes
Skirrs as so many cicadas
On endless frills of quaking twigs
Celebrating the communion of rain.

Lean out into bare space
To visualize your salvation above,
Conjoined to moisture below,
Crossing a season of dust,
An eternity of want
In this blue-gray haze,
Clasping its rattling promise
To wet his good earth, barren,
Yet rich in dry grasses and hope.

ERN
ILL

Now that this low nimbus
Breathes vitality into his soul,
This one, who scales the creaking derrick
Becomes an actor in fate's drama,
Nearer to dizzying heights
Of a world more often than not
An empty chalice laid down,
Rather than a full cup
Lovingly he has feathered the blades
Sighing in their gentle rumble
As the damp air
Brings a moment of promise
To wash away despair and grime.

"Thank you dear Lord great Power Almighty Maker of all things Savior in our hour of need Father Mother Spirit divine Omnipotent Messiah whose name is the One the All the Great Being whose realm is the sky within which your hand directs our life force that is water." "Amen"

God and water become confused in Texas. Man will chant to all manner of forces, knowing little or nothing of the truth.

Storage

Folks secrete these pleasant surprises,
Just around the bend of a road,
Hidden in some corner of their yard,
Some lodestone dangling,
Different, unique, like that old stave church
Built by a possessed artisan,
Never repeated in quite the same manner.
He flung his adze into a lake.

There is always time for eccentrics,
For gifted variations from the norm,
Eight-sided storage sheds in this case,
A small glory, through some alchemy
Blooming in the most unlikely place,
Next door or down that driveway
When mud and country dust
Alternate with the weeks.

Crowned by a cypress tank
Pressing down on its tenon joints,
And mortised for endurance,
All this weight hovers above
Such tools and barrows
As mingle with the children's wagons,
Hoes and rakes in the apse of this temple,
This chapel of artifacts, this joss house
Closeting the spirit of individuality,
Pricking the imagination to wonder,
What special entity is this?
This place of storage.

No ordinary journeyman here.
This is a requiem for skills
All too often lost.
We have our dams, our high steel towers,
Bridges spanning estuaries,
But think for a moment on this,
There are no stapled rattling sheets,
No whizzing bandsaws,
It is not stamped or plicated;
The edifice was crafted.

It was born, created, board by board,
Joist, eave, and rafter,
Patiently shaved, filed and fitted,
Matched and sanded
The grain of old proud forests
Compacted in that seasoned timber,
Holding tightly to the heartwood
Once again, together, in superb function
From the foundation, quaint, octagonal,
To that hoisted tank, cool, banded,
Secure—sheltering its source.

How does it feel to transcend utility?
What song does dame Progress hum
That has more allure
Than the stanzas of an artisan's love?
Moths cling to its weathered sides,
Pigeons strut, jays shriek,
Cats laze in the sunlight,
Children clank their pails,
Carry buckets to the fretful hens,
Or drag an old tire to be hoisted
Swing-wise from some limb.

Revelation wraps itself about
Odd-sided hutches,
From winter's frosty glaze
Summer things retire,
Yet it patiently sits out
Each season's alteration
Reliving its destiny
In this wooded embrace.
Who among us would tinker this shed?
What jaded eye could visualize
Its completion in a world
Where any roughhewn box
Can be dragged or pushed
To an offcorner or enclosure?
There is a sensitivity for all
To find empathy with the happening
Of little things well made.
There has to be a murmur of admiration
For this humble creation.
Someone cared enough to create
A place of storage.

Fort Phantom Hill

Three seasons camped the young dragoons,
Thrust to manhood on these western shields,
Bow-taut, strung by distant hunting grounds,
Phantom horsemen choosing battlefields.

Nearby the Brazos gathered precious rain
So seldom felt among the midden fires,
Where lodgepoles danced in fitful prairie gusts,
The longknives raised their rows of smoking spires.

Not one inscribed; no cenotaph could say
With more emotion 'here was folly known',
'A spot so desolate all hope dissolved',
'An apparition citadel—alone—alone.'

As soldiers will, when ordered, buckle up,
Swing to their mounts, cinches tight, in line,
March out in double file to destiny
Borne on coup sticks, spear, or arrow's whine.

To endless nights upon the sentry mound,
To endless morning peering into glare
Shrinking bald horizons to some hill
Obscured by heat waves in the noonday air.

Then afternoons of torpid, dull routine,
Hauling water to the barrack door,
A brotherhood of volunteer names
Fade into remnants, a misty phantom corps.

They pass the artist's gaze in double file,
Hiyo, hiyo, the petards droop on poles
Hot-clutched to sway in rhythmic canter step,
So brief their time, Fort Phantom Hill's patrols.

Change swept beyond the confines others drew
To separate the clans, both white and red,
Still decades had to pass before that final
Peace evolved on frontiers where they bled.

Powder Magazine, Fort Phantom Hill

Brooding alone, in hulking silence
It waits, hollow and sinister,
The antithesis of destiny,
As ephemeral as memory,
As caught up as milkweed
Sailing by in brief abandon,
A repository of scorpions and spiders,
Commodious vault whose entrance
Admits all, and guards nothing.

We tend to scatter these crypts
All about our history
By the scores, legions buried,
Their contents exhausted
Or abandoned to the elements,
Remaining our remnant companions
In that ragtag parade
Of our passing

So immensely ponderous,
And so brief its hour,
One elongate arch,
A mausoleum attuned to death,
Its thundersticks and powder
Kept a'waiting for some spark
To set free its hoary voice,
Some intensely ponderous
Tumultuous rippling force
Crackling through civilizations
And hordes of barbarians
Bringing down in writhing horror
Twisting adversaries.

A fallen spot of dismal embrace,
Where the hot stab of lancinating pain
Secures that final grimace,
In a chasm of sightless eyes
And mute repositories of orbits
Stripped of their vessels,
Lying about as remnants,
Passing all too quickly into dust.

When the glove of war
Is thrown down in promise
Of conflict pressing life
Into some corner ill-defined,
Some will hurry to a magazine,
Grasp whatever means are hidden
In that dark forboding chamber
Bring it out into the sunlight
And ply the trades of war.

That is the force of survival,
That is the final resource,
Stacked in the stony round,
A museum of emptiness,
Near the Brazos.

School and Barracks, Fort McKavett

Goosenecked spurs their jingling rowels displayed,
Were high strung tinkling chimes among these walls,
Within San Saba's shallow canyons green
With copses brushed by vibrant bugle calls,
From bluff to rifle pits the trumpet's blare
Disturbed remudas where their pawing mounts
Of war awaited curry brush or stiff parades,
A chrism cast on war's baptismal fount.

This was the jeweled pendant of all forts,
Astride a line defenseless, so oft breached
By groaning wagons moving ever west,
Where bison roamed the prairie's awesome reach,
So brief a moment 'til our nation's woe
Recalled their saddled rounds in conflict's name,
What house divided weathers fatal storms?
What balm relieves a populace aflame?

When conflict ceased both victors and their foe
Returned with skills honed razorsharp in hell,
Bluecoats tossing dapper Kossuth hats
Turned full into a tide of rebel yells,
McKavett's square once more felt trooping boots,
More sightings stung the inclined target hill,
Thick capes and greatcoats buffeted by winds
Of change full-brushed their piping, scarves, and drill.

Thus came the orders,
Scrolled on crackling wires,
A last movement,
Pushed on when meaning
Found its zenith.
Civilians filtered in
To opportune their lot
With abandoned retreats,
So it passed; each in its turn,
New life for old,
Barracks to school,
School into history,
A continuum of parades.

San Ygnacio

Valley ribbons flow when mountain thaws
Pulse, then diminish, trickling through its sands,
Escaping to some depth below the scrub
Attuned to desert wasteland's harsh demands.

Fiercely migrant peoples passed in turn
To ride these foothills scarcely tamed,
Awaiting pillage when Comanche moons
Outlined the frontier all too oft inflamed.

Sharp lances chipped the wattle jacal walls,
In times of conquest on their prancing steeds,
Whose warriors in warpaint grasped tight rawhide reins,
Reliving glories of their deadly creed.

From lifeless arms were snatched the hapless babes
Whose chill adoption set them on a course
Erupting as some stream outflows its banks,
Where pity has no father, only force.

Tierra despoblada, fortress home,
Stone to eave to lintel carved and placed,
A living framework pressed upon its soul,
Survival in that courtyard, stone embraced.

What widow lays her head on softest down
When terror rides upon those muffled hooves?
What tides foam down upon her hidden strand
Eclipsed by prairie centaurs on the move?

For them impassioned concepts soon evolved,
Survival from such predatory clans
Seeking beasts or treasures stored within,
To salvage precious remnants, one commands.

Where crumbling plaster clung to weathered stones,
A sundial pointed from one creaking gate,
Announcing with its shadow passing time,
Junctures when more lives would dissipate.

Ygnacio, a stage for friend and foe,
Where night was morbid with its dreadful sounds
Of violent siege upon that narrow world
Locked up within the battlements and grounds.

So palpable the fear when bars were placed,
As rumor followed rumor through that brush,
Each sunrise found some kneeling by a shrine
Whose candles flickered on the Virgin's blush.

Franciscan fathers tilled within the wakes
Conquistadores had rent, whose chattel crept
As skulking grubbers near the mission gates,
Close to the pot, but not the chapel step.

Vaqueros pressed their cattle further north,
Nueces, then Medina, jacquimas
Trooped longhorns through such border towns in droves
That blended soon within that prickly bosk.

Rivers pierced the mustang plains afar,
Now gently seething as the lines were drawn
Between latifundistas, feudal lords
Soon brought to agony as fated pawns.

How many flags were hoisted in the square?
How many bristled at Hidalgo's cry?
How loomed the gringo at the plateau's edge?
Dark omens simmering in a darkened sky.

Again the fractious armies moved as one,
Be civil war or conquest, deadly fray
Dissolved that fragile peace that scarcely bloomed
Among survivors of each war's decay.

Disorder spawned a yearning for those skills
We use to patch the tattered shroud of war,
This reliquary fort held to those dreams,
That clung to life above the battle's roar.

The artist's gaze sought out yet other passing parades
Where horse and wagon, carts aligned that noisy, dusty street
Of wayward commerce caverangos brought to ford the banks
Of wayward rivers cursed by rigmen flailing at their teams,
Of sunburned horsemen cinching barbs tied up before that door
Whose creaking access guarded needs and luxuries scarce known
Before some drummer spread his wares about the counter edge
New fabric yet to feel a blade; new shiny blades to hone.

The needles, combs, armitas, spurs, basins, bits, and boots,
Hung somewhere where the russet tile echoed busy heels,
Those pecked staccato notes with the sighs of maids echoed
Young maidens tagging matrons and a thousand youthful squeals
Of squirming urchins darting past the portals where in time
They too would strut with leather chaps flapping thongs
Tied to their milieu that bound them all within confines
Of San Ygnacio, the fort, the store; a tale prolonged.

Prolonged because that ancient stone in patient homage stands
Protective as this nameless home, a hearth hot with fire
That burns into each youth who kneels where ashes fall,
Symbolic from the day of birth to Charon's final pyre,
Emotive are such times within, be love or turning points
Of lives brought into blossom or decay,
It stands, a remnant, yet in dignity it strains to cry,
"Remember this your humble womb of stone, stick, and clay."

VELA

View

You are lost in this old seabottom,
Set down in solitude as deep as any whaledive,
Palpable in its immensity,
Space measured in heartbeats, anticipation,
Space merged with itself that thrusts
Outward with an order near infinity,
Unknown until experienced,
Unrelieved until puny man
Strode along gentle slopes
Or the other, drawing outlines.
Staring out into nothingness,
And everything-here they set it down,
View, two stores, alone, awash
In calcareous deposits and dust,
A bay or inlet without cephalopods,
Unless the petrified carcass
Of some old Permian beastie
Reminds the passerby of all
Crinoid ancestors; the sinkhole of life
Pressed down, shifted, lifted, displayed
For our brief sojourn, a view.
Well named View, place being
A stopping off, jumping off fulcrum,
A point drifting without hesitation
Collecting the wherewithal
To run herds, springpole a well,
Stock nails, sell weeviled feed,
Here is the calico prairie, a sweep
Of land, sweep of rock, sweep of grass,
A great scattering of the firmament
Where distant movement can descend upon you,
A horizon crashing in,
A gentle undulation of earth titans,
A convulsion of old latitudes, shifted up
From their equatorial plane.
God smithed a doubletree, hooked it to Texas,
One clasp joined here, roundabouts.
Long before primal man peered out
From a thornbush, to think,
Before real thinking man arrived,
Long before the cauldron of evolution
Brought down giants lumbering about,
Sunk to their massive knees,
Leaving View for future epochs.
As we see it, as the artist ruminated,
As a personal filament bound about, entwined
For our moodbeing, for our perusal, for thought,
That so many views are fleeting,
Their counterpoise the incessant erosion
Of what was, is, and seems to be

Tells us there is glory and a weariness
In such space; a nagging doubt
That the essence of our existence
Must be success, in a rainbow of standards.
Here it does not matter.
There is only the certainty
Such places existed, breathed, palpated
With activity, had their day in the sun,

Echoed with curses and prayers,
Creaked in the winds, smelled of ashes,
Blinked in the dust, and for a finale,
Stood alone, center stage,
That last aria sung in near silence,
View became a faint whisper,
Drawn upon this page, a whisper
"This lived also, one place among many."

POST.OFFICE . VIEW . TEXAS

Rochelle

I hear your endless whistle
Blowing hard across the land,
A distant engine steaming
On the Fort Worth-Rio Grande.
For it's New Rochelle, or Old Rochelle, or Rochelle spread
before
Its dusty street, its dusty feet, the barbershop or store,
Those coke fires at the smithy and pale smoke in curlicues
Uplifted tongues of scarlet flame within its sooty flues,
It prospered ever briefly,
As a peregrine in flight,
Sank down into its habits,
Awaiting dawn or night.

Past the flyways of our travels when such migrant hopes
entrain,
Wait the townships barely viable astride some dusty lane,
Lay the Rochelles all about us, their promise scarcely
wrung
From those distant fields around it, man's primeval orison.
Prayers enough for ample harvest when fallow land turns
fair,
Thick with fruiting buds, stamens gossamer as angel hair,
Mornings scented with green clover or thin rows of drying
hay,

Noondays slowed to torpid murmurs in the furnace of each
day,
Sundowns tangerine and purple glowing all about the
dome,
Gleaming in bright cloud embankments footed on the
furrowed loam.

We abide our fateful longing for effort to endure,
Rochelle, the gift, the glory, our despair, and sinecure,
Your battered tin, your tower, clapboard fronts, and tall
facades,
Slimy stockpens, sooty smithy, stately inn, and
promenades,
School in ceaseless small mutations, churches thrust into
the sky,
And the haunted lonely rounds of the watchman's weary
eye.

Towns are cradles, tourney hippodromes, the jousting
courts of man,
A place where merchants count their pence awaiting
caravans,
That humble hallowed hollowness of rusticating knaves,
That mimicry of growing up to ponder on the grave,
Those endless small frustrations where shoeless offspring
run,
Those eerie crossroad whistles, and distant thumping guns,
Where steel hoops crunch on gravel and traces slap on
flanks,
A penurious vale of barter rimmed by creaking sidewalk
planks,
In those lyevat washday cauldrons boiling country grime
away,
We sense a timed but timeless cycle night to silvered day.

What minor contests lost or won, what were the battles
fought
Among the victors, victims, flushed or pale, glad or
distraught?
Within this solitude the artist holds our thoughts to bear
Full face about, to see our past—Rochelle, the town was
there.

It was, and is, and could, and will, and should be, what it
seems,
Such places hold their essence; brute life and sheltered
dreams.

Male Sanctuary

It is kiva quiet,
Still as the mind of one
Who broods in silence,
Wrapped about in thoughts
Inverted by habit,
Shared as a boon,
He senses warm rays
Of that solstice sun
Whose solitary rejoinder
Beams along a marble ledge
Where green liniment glows,
Glints in cheerful abandon,
Its cool spectrum flows
Along the mirrored image
Of the sanctuary.

Soon will be one who joins
That brotherhood beyond
Exposed and breezy streets,
Mornings embroiled in motion,
He has adjusted the cloth,
Swung the chair about,
Lit is the flame beneath a steamer,
The towel is scrolled,
The strop slapped and dangled,
Aromatic wisdom splashes on cheeks
Still smarting from the honed ridge
Stroked so often in an elliptic
Twisting motion; smiles exchanged,
Solemn moments communed,
Assurance of continuity is blessed
In a snipping fashion.

There is tapping of feet,
A silent trickle of hair tufts,
Certain truths are noted, in unison,
Tucked away from benedictions,
Avoiding trilling tongues,
Awash in guilt and browfever,
Awaiting balm from prying eyes,
Seeking likeminded scamps
Now grown, finding their solace
In the male sanctuary
All things are possible.

BER
OP

What Mithraic cellar
Held sway the proselytes
Whose revelations,
Passed on, man to child?
Rites of passage hung round
In the exchange enjoined.
The artist saw those impressions,
Alive in the tonsorial kiva,
He of the clicking scissors
Guarded the old ones,
Tended that secret society,
Where tales were doubly spun.

Gawking siblings kicked the slatted chairs,
Their first haircuts initiation rites,
Where tender early growth
Was dropped ceremoniously by the anchorite,
One whose phrenologic power felt
Each bosselated curve, from man to son,
As sure the architecture of the skull,
As certain was his shrewd comparison,
This, the archive chamber, misty with cologne,
Forbidden bower where dark thoughts were aired,
Longhouse of the tribe where worried braves
Attended their myths about the barberchair.
In our age we laugh, but where do we go
For our mysteries?

Civic Rivalry

There, across the field, are glances,
Each hero pads to some place where glory
Awaits, in the dusty contest of the species,
The contest! It is the contest that enlivens,
It, the contest reaffirms ages of combat,
It is the game, pure, played well, atoning for defeat,
The chance to snatch the laurel wreath again,
A moment envisioning final plays, shouts, and whoops,
That momentous triumph of a high score,
It is the game that fevers this diamond,
It is the rivalry spelled out in the play,
A theater boosted by all, and in that final inning
All will have been said and done.

How like pacing colts whose clatter
Lightly vibrates packed and trampled clay,
Rimmed in lime whose apex is some sack
Sought out among blithe spirits whose melee
Soars when cracking bat connects the hide,
Stitched leather-tight to spin into oiled gloves
Wrenched high or low to grasp in eager palms,
As skill ascends those jostling kicks and shoves,
Egged on in raucous mayhem as the screams
Connect with breathless moments swiftly brought
To firm completion in the thwacking clip
A spinning missile sounds when safely caught!

Where, but to the mound,
All squinting eyes are drawn,
He is Apollo,
And this, the dawn.
Southpaw savant lip curled
Coiled and beadyeyed,
He believes
All things lurk
Within his sleeve,
Secret signals are unfurled
Where he's at,
Spun to lift
Beyond the bat.

In fatalistic rhythm gods redeem their meddling ways,
One inning-two-flyballs-stuck on tortured plays,
Where shortstops stretch arachnid-limbed to snare
That hurtling grounded skipping lump of glare
Smacked across fielded darting testy lumps of men
Howling epithets at every whim,
From bleachers clamor fades when runs are lost,
And tempers rise when orbs are tempest tossed.

When all seems lost, to youth, the bat is passed,
One lucky swing that leaves the field aghast,
Hard by the plate where catchers squat, intent
Upon the losing players loud lament
That song of lamentations rends the air
While others softly swear.

Dust devils swept by players matching skills
So many learned when knuckleballs were thrown,
Where grounded infields lapsed a sure defence,
And outfields stretched to where dry hay was mown,

Loud thumps of horsehide on the catcher's mitt,
Attuned to foul tips longing for the prey,
To tag a hapless runner scarce from third,
His arching triumph, man and ball astray.
Astray from shortstop, centerfield, or first,
Or second—moving in a studied sprint,

Tyro matching master on some move
As cleated shoes templated sharp imprints.
Persuade the Muse of Chance once more to spy
Upon such mortal excess as this game,
Beyond the dull routine of mundane moil,
Circling e'er so briefly Chance's flame,
Remand the loaded bases to our prayer,
This field reminds us; we contested there.

Then momentous triumph, higher scores,
Exultant voices rise above diamond dust,
The rivalry matures to its crescendo
A theater boosted by all, and in that final
Inning-act-movement-division-effort,
All will have been said and done.

Our recollections dance about this leaf
Imprinted by the artist's hand who held
A bat of ashwood clutched in youthful prime,
The joy of play when friendship was compelled
To meet upon the hallowed ground of Game,
In turn his heirs will gamely seek
That ancient resolution teams untangle
Knowing that another chance will occur
To even the score.
This is the gametime where the winner sows
And reaps rewards with clever throws.

Mystical Nomads

Only a child absorbs calliope sounds
As coral polyps strain a shallow sea
Of diatoms; here the nomads rein,
A transitory illusion, just for me.
It was my glory when the carnie Magi
Set up their court of jesters, dwarfs, and knaves,
Their sagging halls of oily canvas tents
Sunk in the sandy alkali by battered staves.

"When I walk the track then cross that shallow ditch
My thoughts are multiplied; my soul bewitched."

The octopus flings outward screaming youth,
Those sharing locker halls and steaming gym,
There cling my peers whose voices rise and fall,
Their frenzied features frozen on railrim,
What bedouin would ply this distant route
To bring such wonders to our moody world?
Their wheel that towers far above the town,
And cannon where a silver acrobat is hurled
Into some flapping net, a squirming fish
Who joins those twisted shapes upon the stage
Parading for our doubting eyes to stare,
While beasts stare back from dark and fetid cage.

"I pay my quarter with a parting sigh,
Its last glint lost within the twilight sky."

Some say they ride the shifting winds,
Lateen rigged dhow cocoons on wheels,
Skimming highway crescents prow to aft,
Strutted ribs on creaking, sagging keels.
And so my tender harshness plods within,
In fantasy some mogul perched on throne,
His fief sargassum rife with noise and cries,
The habitat of barker, freak, and crone,
My peers in wild frenetic leaps
And bounds assault the sideshows soon awake,
Whose summons offer such exotic fare,
All dull past my future would forsake.

"Scarcely burnished is my moral shield
Of self, to high adventure, flesh will yield."

This is the pivot point of mind's embrace
Of other worldly tribes whose migrant course
Invades this rank, austere, pathetic field,
To summon far, exotic fare for simple youth,
Theirs is a soaring tedium, romany genes
Loosed upon a stultified world,
Their only bondage is to cling to self,
A cheerless season like all those before.

That carnie resurrection fanned my fear
That they held powers we ne'er used or sought,
In ignorance of their speech and shaman arts
Our questions came to naught.

"Cotton candy scented dusty air,
As saccharine as the midway glare."

Seconds formed eternities so dark I peeked
Into their hunched lives, set back in booths,
Slouched like spineless dolls upon the stage,
Pale habitat, a flapping world devoid of roofs.

What lie or truth must homeless dross believe?
How are romantics caught in tales untrue?
As mountain trappers sought their pelts before,
What are these fractious goals, what rendezvous?

Nomads raise their calloused palms, itching, ever tingling,
As auric coins rained down on Danae's couch of love,
What silver goes into their purse is slowly won
By whirling tossing countryfolk above.

"Nomads are dark Sufi forming caravans,
Rolling as tumbleweed, blown into our lives."

"They are the essence of Vishnu, returning in their course,
To reappear after some sunset, before some dawn,
Between the mystical hours of owls and dew."

Carson and Barnes Circus

Someone in paint is there,
Someone with tinted hair,
Someone alive in flight,
From bar to swing upheld
By circus spell,
Cathedral tent and mahout acolyte.

Bright posters cling to barns and splintered poles,
Broadleaf promises of old,
Detrained into the circus group,
Beast by beast whose roar
Seeks to restore
A racing hippodrome, a frenzied world spellbound.

Enchanted how our magic-hungry eyes hope to seize
Beneath bright levant canopies
Their painted smiles, and wrinkled pachyderms
Whose solid patience reaffirms
Our dream parades, onward, single file.

Upon such ponderous back the howdah rests,
To rock its lovely guest
Who smiles in turn, with ostrich fan,
Her dimpled cheeks so fresh, fairy mime,
That moving swaying shrine,
Towed by Carson's band.

The rings await
Some steady gait
Parading round about as fancies soar
Into the hurly burly ferment; there, the ark,
Carson's tented show; set within this park,
Menagerie exotic, scarce tamed, upon our shore.

How like a roving army's hungry move,
The creaking wagons, clattering hooves,
Footpads where the tiger's pug sets down,
His slinking crouch and baleful eye
Seeking out our constant cry,
Fearing fatal accident.

Judged to happen, soon, when puny man
Or maid with quiet command
And crackling whip inspire
Tawny predators to roar, great cats
Propelled in graceful leaps from mats
To sway in regal honor high above.

As if this tension could assuage
Terror, taut within that cage
Blaring trumpets tumble those
Buffoons and jesters in whose hearts
Is pandemonium, fits and starts,
From sagging pants to bulbous nose.

Where are their gardens, ballrooms, schools,
Their quiet verandas, evensong, and teas?
Those are their dreams, their wonderment at us,
They are the ships, and we, the restless seas.

Carter Brothers No. 5

Torn from its rails, a spirit of steam seeks rest,
Sunk down in weeds that toss about its crest,
Now rusting, granulating in this grim metallic fate
Reserved for all giants,
Alone, still defiant,
Awaiting the coupling, the agonized tug of some freight,
No longer in tandem strung out in a lifeline of cars,
One engine whose meaning was service to those passing
through,
A burdensome rumble of cylinders fired to their peak,
Through afternoon squalls or droplets of wet morning dew.

What do you signify mostly immersed in forgetfulness,
Some blur of ribbons of concrete astir?
Such blaring intent,
Distorting foment
Crying out to this mammoth "what lies in that cold
sepulcher?
When stoked coals were roaring and steam billows spewed
on ties
At depots united with luggage and hastened goodbyes?"
A point still of reference when children gawked at those
wheels,
Awaiting mutations of motion ascending in squeals,
Behemoth, exciting a hundredfold waysides whose shores
Echoed piercing whistles,
Awaited in drizzle
That ran from your stack in streams in a splattering
wheeze,
Those roaring farewells, like leaves
Swirling in gusts that swooped from the undulant hills,
Echoing mockingbird fifes or the sad whippoorwills.

Vines cling as cobwebs enclosing through life the specter of
death,
Once forged, all leviathans seek out with soot-laden breath
Inhaled, in expanses where crews were alert to stampede,
Or trestles ablaze, or red lights to heed,
Some warning afar,
Or a raildoor ajar,
Where strange shapes peered out, eyes aglow
At the wonder of hoarfrost or snow,
That signature, Five, tugged some circus along in its wake,
Past thicket strewn bayous or reed bordered lake,
Until on this siding, passed up, fate muffled its roar,
It waits, but hears not that call, ne'er to be; nevermore.

Dumbly, as all foundry horses go dumbly to serve,
Where the pointing of rails deviates on each twisting
curve,
Your infinite joy was a cargo of imagery set
Down in the rings,
Those live, throbbing rings,
White geldings in slow pirouette
Performed, long accustomed to noisy, ebullient cheers,
Awaiting the circus in simpler, more emotive of years,
So, buttressed by vines forgotten old relic, you lie
Embraced in pitiless winds and an uncaring sky.

Vulcan Calmed

Igneous womb, the hot furnace glow, its fire,
Annealed by pressures from which magma pours,
A river of iron squeezed out from searing spouts,
To boil in agony across some hot sintered floor.

We grew on steel bands nailed fast to oak, laid as ties,
Sight leveled broad tiers as levees of fine gravel beds,
Those forges of Vulcan blazed hotly with primal intent,
To meld hardened fabric from spark hammered threads.

We grew, my lame forgemaster god, in the wills of our land,
Not from gold that our destiny chose for such functional plates,
Drilled hooplike with boltholes that tied the dark metals fast
About your raging red soul that lapped at white glowing grates.

In quiet isolation you erode in this slow bitter pyre,
Each droplet consumes what was born in a river of fire,
Just the artist, a drawing, and memory fading in time,
And a few words arranged in four stanzas of rhyme.
The power of change is the power to cease to exist,
A discarded relic soon blurs in a distant, gray mist.
In the flurry of change what is will be destined to past
And the greatest of treasures will be destined seldom to last.

NORTH ZULCH

Depot, North Zulch

There's the little station, just as I
In youthful parody of manhood left
Its cramped confines, it whispered
"Go, desert this tattered village
Where pain was norm, so much hope
Expired in drab captivity,
Where most toiled and few held promise
That indifferent and faded joys would be,
Reward for being born."
This tiny enclave set aside, waiting
That brief moment which the whistle
On steaming cold mornings promised,
Whose summer steam formed more dew,
Whose autumn tailwind twisted the bag
Of mail suspended in its formless silence
Upon its pole to be ensnared as much as I
Was caught in a remnant village, alone.

No Andean slope knew more of solitude
Than youth encased within a void,
A flask whose stopper poised alone this track
Awaiting its release; each train was promise,
It left, a worldly promise that beyond,
The Zulch of anxiety, the Zulch north or south,
A place evicted from the minds of all
Who placed the last harvest, the last valise
Upon the depot ramp, to set free the genie
Trapped within that brushy bottom, those fields,
To hear those doors thump close, to watch the treasure,
Youth, the ones afoot, slip away, in a cloud of steam.

Old depots twist in the wind, they stand
In the path of progress, roads, crossings,
Forgotten by rusting engines in fallow meadows,
Swept away as any debris, by change.

Waterstop

The days were broken by hours
Swept up in a blanket of wind,
Where darkness contrasted with sunshine,
And time was a wheel scarcely spinned,
We looked to the edge of creation,
In the finite infinity sky,
Awaiting some distant procession,
A wailing most plaintive impression,
Evoking my longing for movement,
For a train that would never reply.

An oasis of water upended,
Its pipe gently swaying above,
Teasing rollblanket clouds dark with moisture,
Where every cool shadow is loved,
Pattering droplets of water
Dripping down on a range never plowed,
Awaiting some enginehiss motion,
Those violin wires in this ocean,
Strung lengthwise along rusting tracks,
Where dust was a billowing shroud.

It waits on thick pillows of cypress,
A galvanized promise of steam,
Whose spout rattles softly in cadence,
Suspended on splittwisted beams,
What engineer failed to acknowledge
A respite upon empty runs,
A spectral train without rumble,
When pistons devoid of their rumble,
Are lost in a lie most explosive,
In the roar of its anthracite sun.

Blazevibrant, eclipsing coronas,
What aura is that nimbus of fire?
Its energies burned in our conscious
Reflections of former empire.
Juggernauts cleaving the twilight,
Are remnants that time has withdrawn,
There is only mirage,
Fragmented collage,
A waterstop bathed in the sundown,
A promise forgotten by dawn.

So pungent that odor arising
Where bunch grasses clung to our legs,
Creosoted ties and gum rosin,
Exuding from now empty kegs
Rolled back of that toolshed, forgotten,
Where railgangs would loiter and rest,
When coffee was brewed in the last car,
The rattling red hulk of the last car,
When hot oil in wheelboxes sizzled,
Where starlings flew in from the west.

When kerchiefs were stretched over nostrils,
Where tank water splashed through that bore,
Collecting as all streams must gather,
In the confines of some reservoir,
A transient vapor hangs over
The memory of railmen whose bloom
Dried as petals between yellowed pages,
Pressed and lifeless between dusty pages,
No longer fresh-scented and tossing
Among the bunch grasses and broom.

We press on with our flyways and pavement,
We bypass old fixtures of need,
Our comfort and tempo satiated,
We are that final stampede,
Our trestles have burned, and the grasses?
They sprout whether bison or men
Share time on the unwieldy prairie,
Share grime at the cypress-lined aerie,
Where old relics clutch yet to their footings,
Eroded, corroded, in gritbreeze and malodorous winds.

Point Isabel Lighthouse

Dark lagunas are born in the tideflows,
Where river and seas vie for space,
To spew up white crystalline sandbars,
Captured and briefly embraced.

Here barrier levees survive from the onslaught of winds,
Blown foamfrothy puffed in the salient violence of djinns.

Sea djinns stirring waters oft troubled,
Which flail at the quivering strands,
Once lonely in flat isolation,
Bemused by Poseidon's commands.

What conch blasts disturbed busy flyways
That stretched below subtropic sun?
Be they dugouts or shrimpboats or lighters,
They were prey as were rich galleons.

In treachery born, oft conceived in the violence of spheres,
Storm tides are a litany writ in the matrix of fear,

Rubbed raw are the nerves of old seamen,
Immersed in that deep inky night,
Seeking a sign, some faint glimmer,
One brazier whose scintillate light,

Whose flickering promise is safety,
When the saltladen breath of the djinns
Flap rigging and sheets in their fury,
That cold scream of force peregrine.

Seafarers pray for pale beacons and bellbuoy sounds
To guide them to quays far removed from hungry sea
hounds,
That snap at the tillers and bay in the fastness of hell,
Rare comfort from rays of a lantern, or soft distant bell.

By degrees on the Rio de Palmas,
Caribbean borne vapors in transit
Blew gulf sailors close to the headlands,
Compass nibbed by wet dripping bowsprit.

All courses steered fast on that lodestar,
A white column tended and shined,
A crystalline lens held high
Above sand haze of moisture and brine.

Pale shepherdess thrust by resacas
Casts shadows as would a sundial,
To mark on that solar horizon
The bounds of a desolate isle.

The artist has tramped on those wet decks by gunwales
well worn
Where the dark pitchstained snares of strong webbing
successively borne,
Sank down into fathoms for nekton who dimly perceived
Silhouettes of their fate in the meshes of nets, heave by
heave.

Past the twilights he peered ever westward to seek in that gloom
Some beacon that glimmered so dimly, so faintly on spume
Tossed about in the saline expanse of those channels he knew,
Fast tethered to lights on the inlets, or backwater slough.
Now distanced from use in the silted deep runnels of time,
That unblinking shepherdess stands fast in her pasture of brine,
Here crustaceans dig ever so spritely between fairy waves
Ensconced in wet sticky fine sifted grit swirled to their caves.

Dissolved in a timemist miasma sea memory soon fades
From processions of shipmen and menships whose pillar did last
As the zodiac points on the cusps that precession evolves
A lighthouse whose comforting nimbus in time too would pass.

This point marked for decades in silence shrugs naught at its fate,
Not now will this remnant be sought by those far behind
A shifting dune barrier transforming with seasons of change,
The cyclops stands weary, bypassed, its great lenses blind.

Lighthouse, Harbor Island

Lazy boat tooling on the lazy waters, yo.
Lazy day heating e'er so gentle, e'er so slow,
Bait bucket smells as all bait buckets do,
In a line with the markers and the lighthouse too,
Now the ripples tell of mullet and I know from the skies
That white pelicans seek with their yellow rimmed eyes
Silver fishes scooped up in a sagging pouch beak,
Those same finny flashers that the seagulls seek,
Soon other plopping outboards will sputter on the bay,
In line with the tower whose light passed away,
Whose eye lost its gleam as all relics do,
Awaiting my passage to our wet rendezvous.

A meeting in the shallows where the redfish swim,
In the rim of the glim as the sea terns skim,
Find me making ripples where the green duck grass
Lies plashy quaggy thick in sight of the pass,
Let idle moments stretch and meander with the sun,
Rolling up hazy shadows when the poor mullet run,
Like a gray blue heron I will bask in that light
To fish 'til the darkness of the pale twilight.

With a tense reel humming jaws snap on the bait jerking
there
In the shallows, light has failed, light is gone.

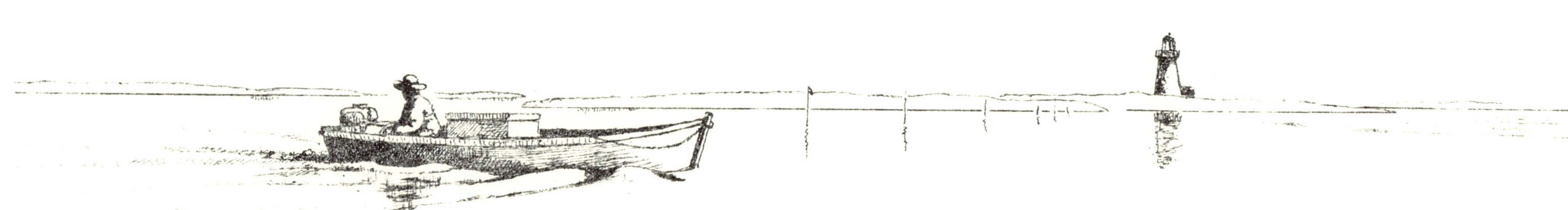

Soon moored postwise, my skiff will rest,
Beneath pale flyways lit by moon,
So far from granite scoops of northern lakes,
Removed from testy grebe and mournful loon.

That unlit column had no broad causeway,
Its hermit trolled a ferment scented slough,
Kneedeep sunk down in the muckwet sludge,
Companion of the gull and billed curlew.

With simple lines the artist drew my course,
Putt plopping sputter thumping on and on,
My ruddy skin burned by a constant glare,
Myself a mystic, gray old tired heron.

Lazy aboat tooling on the lazy water, yo,
Soon to drift on the 'madre's flow'
Where rust peppered barges find the channel's edge,
And islands form near a bucket dredge,
One sad light stands,
One heron peeks
There quickly
Thrusting beak,
Below,
Caught in a timeless, timeless flow of those that swim
or fly or plop scud sputter as me; old crusty me, beneath
that avian chatter lost in the magic swirl of tide and sky.

Lane to Sisterdale, Badenthal

Crackfire summer solstice heat pours as a river of sound,
Cicadas sing to bubbling waters rushing past the mound
Obscuring cypress naves thrust from banks line on line,
Cathedral creeks whose silver flow like unravelled twine
Dash Guadalupe bound writhing on the valley floor,
Two Sister Creeks converging beyond that schoolhouse
door,
Where fieldstone and gold quarry blocks remain, a legacy
Hauled there by oxen yoked, their destiny.
Debating clubs in ferment when rebellion sparked their
zeal,
Or ground their weak resistance beneath some tyrant's
heel,
Desire for freedom their intent, dissent their heinous crime,
Disease and disappointment lurking past the maritime.

Torn again in civil conflict, rode they blue or gray,
Adrift within a tragic storm of hardship and dismay
That plumbed the depths of dark despair; such numbness
few believed
That hope would salve the emptiness of mankind thus
bereaved,
This was the smithy of their souls, this hushed and
mellowed scene,
A harvest ripe for scything, fresh stalks for death to glean,
Uncertain precious seedlings cast out upon false grants,
Yet thrusting roots with vigor, by grand design or chance,
Ofttturned the season's colors, green to russet, sere, and
blown,
Scattered in the panic thrusts of a winter's boreal moan,
Gusty herald blasts of northers fanning coals into hot fires,
Ascendent hardships beckoned death as leaves blew
higher, higher.

Soon in frozen desolation rime-glazed fieldstones ashlar set
Reflected wisps of logfire forming sooty coronets,
Naked now the mighty cypress looked down at the freshet
flow,
Frigid ribbons changing hues in the spectral wintry glow,
This the artist could imagine; this evolved in constant
change,
Unrolled as prickly barbs fencing out the open range,
My own reflections passed to verse when on a biting morn
I walked among the ice-bowed weeds and remnant fields
of corn,
Detailed figments of the past appeared within this place,
Days bygone, moments lived, my thoughts sought to
retrace.

Its stiff unyielding stubble crunches keen,
As creaking boots go crackling on light frost,
They scrape rough icy gravel with a growl,
Sharp filigrees of crystal light embossed.

A slanting weakened sun is glowing now,
Yellow limestone blocks outline its eyes,
Those staring frosted windows seeking light,
Reflecting twisted oaks and restless skies.

A fragile cloak of silence sets the mood,
Fingers tingle, cheeks sting from the cold,
My thoughts in scattered reverie are sunk
Into this solitude, a tale retold.

Exhaling frigid streamers I respond
To such an introspective private place,
A whistling breeze rattles stiffened boughs,
And sets my features in its cold embrace.

No smoke is seen to curl above that flue,
This antique room knew decades as it stood
Anachronistic to our present time,
What worth evolved if talk it only could?

My stiffened fingers touch the harness rail
Where horses whinnied, relic of that day
Reminding me how fleeting is the force
Of glaciered time in rebirth and decay.

Broad pathway trod by other smaller feet
In overalls and gingham with tin pails,
Assembled in a cluster, skipping scholars
Hanging caps and bonnets on bent nails.

Squirming, jostling, laughing, cries chaotic,
Every desk an altar for the mind,
Simple basic thoughts upon the chalkboard,
Simple answers on their slated line.

Scratching stylus sounds with rustling leaves,
Coughing spells, the humdrum rapping fingers,
Clanking door, the popping crackling firewood,
Pressing inward where scarce memory lingers.

Horizons lay from ridge to grassy crests,
Rude pleasures blended with their simple fare,
Within this yard their friendships were a strength,
They drank pump water, gladly breathed the air.

So many missed that pealing note of summons,
Infections stripped their ranks as tiny graves
Appeared in scores of small enclosures,
Reminding us, some pass, yet some are saved.

Theirs was an adolescent changing era,
New inventions brought the weight of change,
Fragile tenure on this earth slipped by,
Cotton pushed out longhorns on the range.

Prairie grasses hugged crude rambling fences,
Spiked wire shackled landscapes once held free,
Static lifestyles cramped their pilgrim spirits,
Now wraiths upon a ghostly grassy sea.

Children grew in stature with their siblings,
In time that final teacher locked the doors,
Away they drifted into Texas currents,
Country dust lay thick on country floors.

I stepped into that feeble wintry sunshine,
Strode past the oaks on numb and tingling feet,
To where encroaching blackbirds whirled in flocks
Adding raucous din where waters meet.

How many frosty seasons will this marker
Stand in silence, epitaph to change?
This limestone memory, once a treasured schoolhouse
Lingers, set apart upon that vanished range.

It served its day, so now deserves its respite,
This bonded fossil mass set down in loam,
Quarried, stacked, full chinked as block and lintel,
About those eaves the wind still whispers, 'home'

Wagonshed, Tackroom and Smithy, Badenthal

There is a fusion of man and beast,
Longer running than our recent years,
There, efforts were a partnership conjoined,
Bound to hot machines and scratching gears,
Who in our time remembers legacies
Of hot oiled leather, bits, and shingletrees?

Unyielding iron was transformed in the glow
Of sparkling coal roaring to its flue
As sooty fireflies whose brief moment passed
To drift aloft, man's grimy residue.
In clanging cadence tools were shaped to serve
Work-toughened sinews in those calloused hands,
Bound with leather harness teams pulled out
Among the fields, spurred on by rough commands.

Think, if you will, the patient plodding hours
That spanned each season, hot or bitter cold,
Success or failure rode upon the winds
That only chance controlled.
There was a past that knew more bitter times,
Before the schism Lee and Lincoln shared,
When intellects still stranger to such strife
Pushed on with perseverance, worked and dared.

Dared to form this colony that shone
As brightly as a nova casts its rays
Into uncharted heavens where fears lurk,
And cold reality slays.
It was their glory, brilliant Sisterdale,
This hamlet, rich with talent far beyond
The dull expectations one would find,
Within that dreary frontier of despond.

These drafty confines, humble cypress rooms,
Knotted, shriveled, blotched with grime and oil
Themselves within the confines of stone walls,
A barn, and coachhouse marking yet this trail,
The Pinto trail, a lifeline down through valleys
Upon which redmen and their restless foes
In silent caution passed between the huts
Where grubbed the untried migrants
Forming squares of notched and chiseled logs,
Setting course between their sour dreams,
And fancied gifts, where nature had endowed
Such promise into beauty roughhewn as their hands
Yet long excoriated in excesses known
To all pioneers, all who dared this fragile peace
Set within these enclaves, topped with shingles
Split from river giants, and warmed with prairie growth.
They dressed these massive blocks of stone,
Brought in ideas spreading up the track
Worn rutted, dusty, and soon branched
Where institutions rose and social order
Set its patient roots into the soil.

These were achievers in their finest hours,
Living on this site where this, the tackroom
Waits yet for some form now flown without,
As do all useful relics, remnants of change.

It was the smithy where those pistols born
Of war were crafted for those soon to go,
Never to return, an ancient litany of war,
Names to be dispersed, grieved, and forgotten,
Met briefly in that decade, a roster of so many
Displaced into oblivion, displaced from gaols
Along the Rhine, torn now between lines of men
Whose battleflags rose and fell in that unique
Watershed of our nation's being.

They sang, spoke well, trusted freedom's flower,
Wrote endlessly, loved, and trained their youth,
Were dissipated into history's byways, rose and sank
Into their destiny as echoes some believe can't fade.
Others came in their stead, and life resumed.
How prosaic change; thrust upon tilted backs
As a dusty mantle pressing down on bowed shoulders
Of any wanderer who dares.

This Badenthal, a place of healing waters, gathered those
Of kindred mind milling on this Texas, wild and bellicose.

Of all those structures in this village,
The artist chose these three,
Personifying what survived their highflown
Philosophic paeans and war's debris.

When crackling storms push by,
And roaring ferment tosses leaves
About the stableyard each blinding glare
Becomes a frieze.
A frozen moment pinched between raw cracks
Of older boards than I, whose ancient days
Are less than harness still held on those hooks,
In quiet displays.

Earsplitting thunder shatters inky night
With shadows flitting on the tackroom floor,
Forming wraiths within the smithy shed,
Memories, and little more.

Driving rains pound tin and tear at earth
Where hoofprints long have disappeared,
It is the varmits now who wait it out,
For a chilling moment shapes evolve,
Swirling round thin elms,
Sentry straight above that smokehouse,
Then converged with aimless specters
Just as did pale plasmic forms,
Set in cheerful runs of country labor,
Old men bent and women wracked
With one endearing moment when with love
They fond embraced their kind.

With gusto sweaty triumphs stretched those reins,
The smith and his iron were melded tight
Into some grainy alloy amply struck,
Whose metal fiber held its plastic cast,
In primal heat upon the anvil's plane.
There were no second thoughts,
Mundane drabness was the norm,
Creped along the wall black squirrels
Flicked nervous tails and eyed the sphere,
Here migrants suckled Gaia's bosom,
Meager, scarce rewards were clutched,
And here the ethic handed down, emerged,
Through yeomen pressed upon their plows,
Scything grain whose pregnant sheaves
Fed the master and his beasts.

Badenthal, whose water cure
Presaged more clever balms
Relieving flesh as spirits
Soared with psalms,
This was nature's narthex
Pointed at oath's altar,
Ingenious ones who persevered
And some whose seed ne'er fell,
Here, crystal springs and green banks
Were backdrops for great change,
They drew upon their past,
Transplanting things ethereal,
And more pragmatic works that last.

Such rooms were hubs supporting wheels
Where early lives evolved,
Chapels in memoriam
Of deep resolve.

The storm wound down, passed along within the creek,
Now swollen to a torrent, tossing limbs
Where once the patients soaked their worldly pain,
Where cicadas hum and cypress sings.

When normal is the night,
The tackroom waits,
And smithies dust their ash,
By ashlar gates.

Northside Southside

Flocks in their edgy quest observe
Pale reflections seeped in lake or stream
Or rust-stained tin whose glitter
Closely matches noonday gleam,
They swoop with noisy cries on ridge and vane,
Seeking largess of scattered bits of grain.

For here within this massive, rambling heave
Of storage cribs where harvest is consigned,
Are spaces open as the high staked plains
Through which the harvest winds will loudly whine,
Complaining hinges creak on restless gates,
For man and beast this sprawl of clapboard waits.

This ark, whose cubits match old Noah's craft,
Rides with the seasons not on high Ararat,
But sinks its keel within these uplift seas,
A complex, lonely airy habitat,
This battered hulk whose northside sets the tone
Symphonic as a winter's blast full blown.

Here ice accumulates upon thick moss
That clings to soggy boards about the sills
Whose casements seldom know the passionate sun,
But feels the icy breath of arctic chill,
Northwise ever lurking in deep shade
Glazeslick posts define that trampled prairie esplanade.

Snorting streamers curlicue from muzzles
Steaming in the frigid atmosphere,
Shivers bound across their twitching flanks
Awaiting gear.
They turn full rump about avoiding thrusts
Of algid winds and sleeting gusts.

Cabals will ne'er convene where tractors wait
To churn the mud well-mingled with debris,
No soaring transept here, no gothic vault,
No trefoil arches, glass, or filigree,
Its bounty lies in heaps within that gloom,
That daybreak will relume.

Consumed by work and time barns lack their bards,
What lyrics could a minnesinger weave
About some relic sprawled in disarray?
What notes would he conceive
Inspired by blowing straw or rattling tin,
His fingers stiffened on the mandolin?

Jackets firmed by moisture scarce unbend
As hay is pitched from lofts, molasses poured
And salt blocks set upon the feeder shelf,
Within that moment, winter is ignored.
Dumbly ruminating stock and mounts are free,
In darkest night of bit and whiffletree.

There comes a time
When childhood ventures out from makebelieve,
Awed by immenseness of this alcazar
Whose naked beams and whistling eaves
Are both a fright and comfort now explored
In ever widening fashion board by board.

When mysteries of the northside ceased,
As I grew well accustomed to my chores,
To strengthen limbs of boyhood soon to man,
Those fantasies of childhood years restore
Imaginary fiefs with I, the lord
Defending all with cape and wooden sword.

Newness rose afresh in early Spring,
The southside was a tapestry of birth,
One dwelled in warmth with slingshot well in hand
Defending castle keep and sacred earth,
A scented moist earth, hills to orchard lanes,
Where I trooped waging brief inspired campaigns.

Somedays commotion filled the titan shed,
Squeals from the sty and pigeons by the score,
Up from the southside dogs would add their howls
To drown the tractor's roar,
And clacking shredders scythed that brushy rim
Of tanks within which memories swim.

Strutting roosters sickle tails in motion
Ruled the days with sparrows, wrens and crows,
Yet when the darkness stirred nocturnal hosts,
And banshee movement passed in twilight glow,
A gray blurred hunter swooped in eerie flight,
To rule in silence deepest night.

I felt the rainbreeze in its prime,
The April patterns sown in rapid change,
Droplets rattling snaredrums overhead,
As curtained tempests bent the open range,
Then just as briefly April left the stage
To other actors left for Autumn's sage.

W
S

Lands and Furrows

What monument in other ages hewn
Performed such service as this broken stone?
Wedged from its strata, tipped, and hauled away,
Then furrowed,
As a fallow field,
Alone.

No stele this, exalting long dead kings,
Inscribed with grand designs or sacred verse,
This, the miller's patient drudge has grist
Yellow kernels,
Sacked and soon dispersed.

Close by the millrace or some misty flume,
A chance acquaintance or the neighbor's kin
Draws up the buckboard groaning with its load,
And steps within.
He watches land and furrows use their hour
Shaping harvest grains to meal or flour.

Sacks expand, dust settles on warm gears,
From other valleys stories make their rounds,
Aggressive sparrows peck and flit about,
To add their voices to the millrace sounds,
Land is by the furrows soon caressed,
Grinding sack by sifting sack on the land's largesse.

Abruptly then, the Texas flood bears down,
Ravines full surge, then canyon, valley floor,
Piling debris on the millpond dyke,
Its cheerful aria, now a mighty roar,
Other furrows etch the flinty soil
Of banks despoiled.

Torn asunder shard by splintered shard,
Crushed beyond a shattered hulk it sends
Wet fragments now detached from stones,
Rushing madly down to turgid fens.
Staring from the heights the miller sees
What once was,
And sinks upon his knees.

The remnants? Fractured, long bypassed and rolled
Aside as one would bare a tomb,
Fades from life as did that useful weir
By unrelenting nature thrice consumed.
The dreadful truth is
Taught by tempest stricken crashing rolls,
A voice so full no other cry can be
Annunciating our reward,
Success, then total agony.

In fits and starts
We challenge this, a frightful universe,
Where changes measure short the shrift of God,
And man lies bleached within his garden curse,
Stones are cycled firmament,
Phoenix-like soon pulverized,
Then lifted windward staining faded skies,

All that is left is sand, sea,
Or furrowed land.
And the least of these
Is left to God's remand.

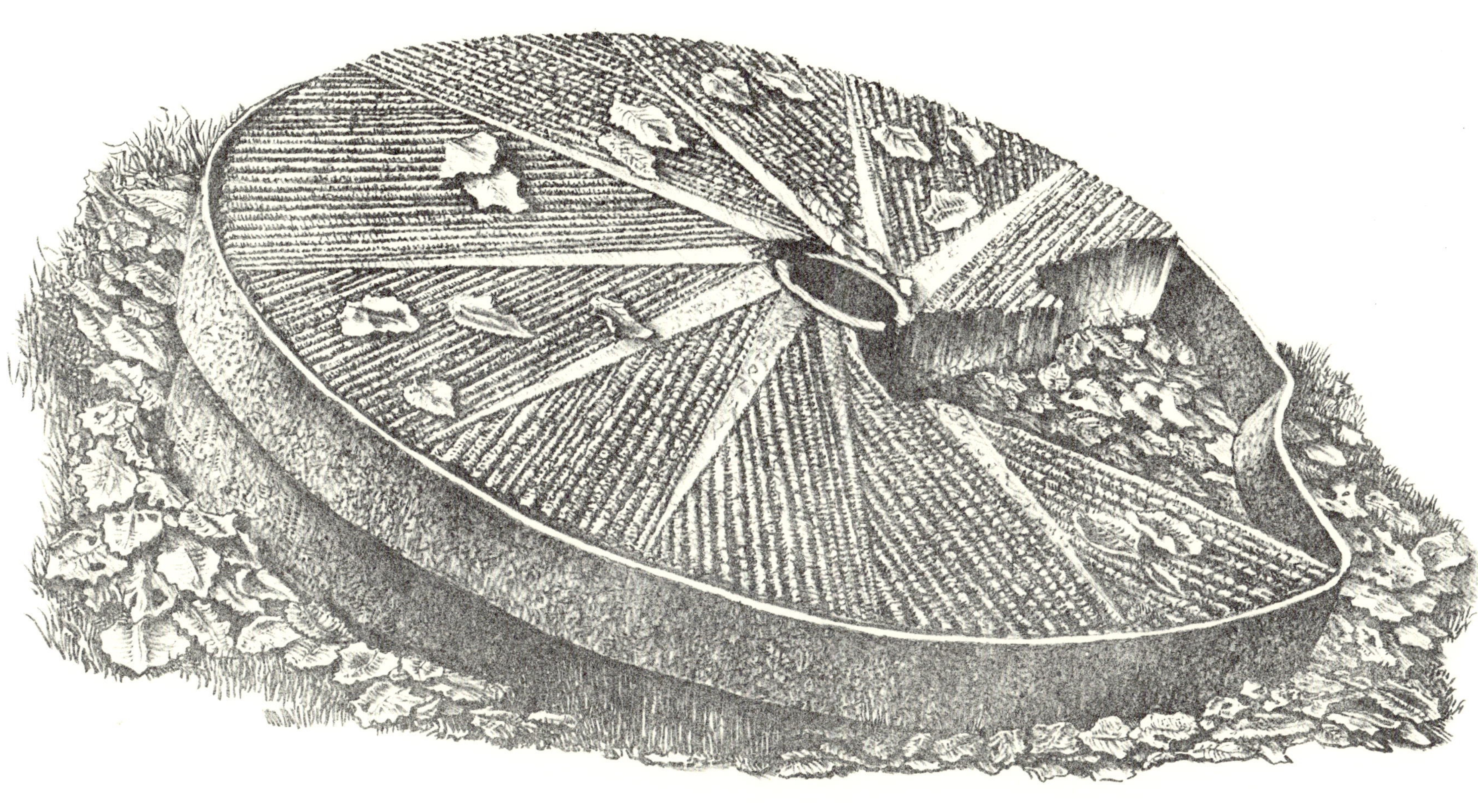

House in Seymour

"On they came, eager pilgrims,
Bent on taming land,
Seeking grubbing room or grazing
Prairie down to sand,
My hallway filled with voices
Seeking shelter from the chill
Insistent gales of roving fronts
Rattling casements on my sills."

"Exhausting treks through distance
Measured in a span whose breadth
Was stamped upon the unborn,
Or ceased in death.
Dusty, grimed or sore from riding
Migrators sought rest within my walls,
Respite from a weary crossing
Seeped in bone dry summer heat, or squalls."

"Upon my steps they slumped in heaps,
Huddled inward, dulled from grim fatigue,
Too numb to cry,
Immersed in timeless space, league on league.
Mile on endless mile
They grasped at any guidepost, sign,
Or promise of a bedding down,
Protected from an elemental whine."

"There were the women, frayed and worn,
A tattered lot whose toil etched deep
Their burnished faces lined and seamed with care
Disturbing sleep,
Aged far beyond their seasons care was a shawl
Wrapped tight as any shroud or linen pall."

"And still the wagons creaked without remorse,
Far inland, dies were cast, all bridges burned,
My hospice was a kindness for brief hours
Where they sojourned.
Yet on occasions, one or two remained,
To pile their markers at the boundary lines,
About some acreage drawn in metes and bounds,
Soon posted, barbed, and close confined."

"Range talk, pallets, straw, and drinking bouts,
The acrid smell of bacon, coffee, beans,
A wedding party trooping up my stairs,
A solemn wake, or country law convened,
Thespian trollops, malcontents, and rakes,
Evangelists whose raptures shook my panes,
Purgatory savants bent on love,
Clutching converts, sinful or profane."

"Most were a decent lot whose eyes were clear,
In time the numbers shrank, the pathways worn,
Soon witnessed horseless buggies, motor drays,
A parody of noise and grating horn.
What haunting memories have my walls embraced?
What fragments of our past are here encased?"

Chores

A play on words

Chores are hand-me-downs, a legacy of doing,
An aggravation of necessity,
Fathered by Arthritis, borne by Soreness,
Chores fungate, well-suited to rusticating arenas
Where all effort is painfully rewarded.

The time is between wars and drought. Two philosophers steeped in leisure approach a sun dappled glade appearing surprised to find cached within this quivering bucolic setting, a milkmaid and her cow. One, an artist, reaches for his pad, purses his lips, and pats his purse. The other—a poet, pats his stomach and lisps his lines.

Artist: "A comely wench whose lines
Are those of fair Diana pursuing Acton,
Methinks her skills far outshine the pail,
I shall enshrine this moment in detail."

Poet: "She hummeth such a ditty, cup your ear
Lest such a melody should filter by,
Those dulcet tones anoint our souls with fire,
Inspired, that rural ditty, 'a blue-tailed fly'."

Artist: "Pray that no creative menopause
Would stay my hand poised to press
Upon this paper precious tribute
Surging within my seminal being
Her eagerness to generate froth from kine
Is an inspiration; relate your soulful tune
Oh Muse of Milk."

Poet: "I could ruminate until it clabbered,
Such poignant recollections filter down of another,
A Delphian sibil perched upon a tripod,
A Cumean sibil aloft in her high sanctuary."

Artist: "She turns our way; her smile
Exposes chill penury; there are more lichens
On those gums that crustate broad oaks, yet
Note a tea-rose glow within her eyes."

Poet: "Rheumy lids, reddened as a sunset,
And those hands?"

Artist: "Scaled reptilian in the coarse pursuits
Of life, bent double over tub and drainboard,
Hers is a harshness tempered not with balms."

She begins to notice the gentlemen observers who appear to keep a discreet distance, a situation influenced by a dense cloud of gnats. The artist straddles a stump. His face is a study of inspired ferment. The poet settles himself gingerly on a convenient nearby mound, an antbed.

Poet: "She seems to speak, but softly. Such a lass was my
mother, toiling in the vineyards of life. How soon one
forgets
these old ways, that perpetual burden of chores."

Milkmaid: "Surely the fury of fireants will change your
poetic meter."

Artist: "My youth flowered among Augean stables,
Aquarius-like my arms ached from pails of water,
With pliant rods I drove the cattle to their knolls,
And with hoarfrost crunching underfoot, cracked brittle ice
Layered fast within the slimy troughs."

Milkmaid: "Two dogs of the road, more entwined with
rhetoric
Than conjoined in useful activities."

Her voice rises as does the poet from the swarming nest of predators.

"We can benefit one another. Would you quit this insect
agora
For a steaming stack of buckwheats?
There are bales of hay awaiting stacking,
And in yonder edifice, a wheel to be reset
Upon the slickened bearings of my manure spreader."

Artist: "Fair indeed, or is it fair Pomona,
Or Ceres? In truth, though we would with delight
Share that checkered cloth of plenty
Draped across the altar of your cuisine,
Even this crayon bears down upon my being,
My creaking spine is a wilderness of petrification,
Bales are baleful, and pails cumber the shoulders,
My body is eternal torment, this poor relic
Lives though memory dimmed in a miasma of drudgery."

Poet: "The arduous campaigns of creativity have withered
Arms and thigh—."

Milkmaid: "But not your jaw—."

Artist: "Cast your gaze more, yes, more to the right,
There, now I have the pose.
So many Vestals have quit the temple,
But here remains one dedicated to hearth and health,
Both feet rooted to this fair soil."

Poet: "We wrap verse about her
As two arachnids spinning gossamer threads,
Let this agile maid, this rural gazelle
In her own vernacular, within her sylvan habitat
Regale us with a recitation of her aspirations."

Milkmaid: "I do need wood hewn,
And those tilted fences—but yet
There is more compost in their words
Than piled in stink about yon shed.
Their simple faces belie crafty intellects.
Much they need to be humored.
If it is the handmaiden of verse they seek,
Then I am their Sappho and this squirting milk
An elixir whose alchemy is a sack of cottage cheese."

Artist: "Your patient ruminant has a name?"

Milkmaid: "Sukey, but like purple, it rhymes with naught."

Poet: "Like mauve, also useless in my trade.
Your blouse is stained but your tongue is nimble.
What other facets gleam within your forest setting?"

Milkmaid: "Work thrives with dusty locks and grimy
skirts.
Your observation foretells my lot,
Much remains to be done before Lethe closes my eyes,
A daily manumission from these, my chores."

Poet: "The manacles of servitude chafe the soul."

Milkmaid: "I discerned a flicker of terror in your eyes.
Drudgery by any other name is just as grubby.
But enough of this parlance.
Country custom dictates that I revert to form,
To my normal diction, to my idiomatic meter,
I must cast away this stilted diatribe,
Enjoin the patois of this region,
Texas speech in style and substance,
In barbecue fashion, down to the meat of the matter."

Artist: "Speak only in the silvery verse of Byron,
Speak now, daughter of servitude,
Child of agrarian seed,
Tiller of loam, nymph of bough and blossom,
Let my eyes feast on such potential—."

Poet: "Let my jaded ears reap the harvest
Of thy verse."

Milkmaid: "This is where it all hangs out, bozos."

HEREUPON BEGINS THE MILKMAID'S POEM.

"This is a far cry from ease,
No lace, furs, silk, fancy china,
No chamber music, morning teas,
This is it—grab a tit and pull,
Afore I'm done, a bucketful."

"Sukey is a rangy cow,
Beats flies about my head,
Flicks her swatter on my brow,
Twitchtailed and monstrous dumb,
Caught between four fingers and thumb."

"'Queen of Utters' some have said,
Queens played at milking, take Antoinette,
But the game went to her head,
Chores fall on us country folks,
Forever the butt of city jokes."

"This artist fellow sitting here
Draws and draws while the streams squitch,
Milk flows in squirts, he seems sincere,
Called me a remnant of change—me?
I'm a better remnant than old Marie."

"Earthfreaks set down here, too,
Back to basics, plows, sows, and cows,
They tramp my garden down to goo,
Then monotony sets into their brains,
And their green enthusiasm wanes."

"If I had my druthers, would I drag
Foamy milk from out this bag?
Not a bit, my girlhood dreams
Are milking machines.
Think on this poet, when you romanticize
Chores, you fantasize.
My verse is choppy, but ten to one
Your milking's sloppy."

Artist: "That nasal twang does not dim
Profound philosophy stretching back to Solon,
This bewitching begonia thrives in this glade."

Poet: "Her presence nips at the nib of my pen,
Yet the atmosphere has a hardened quality to it,
There is a paucity of pancakes,
Her grim subtleties of expression
Indicate that reward follows labor."

Artist: "The hour has arrived to see to advantage
Another treasured sequel in this folio yet enscribed,
Another maiden awaits to be immortalized,
Down that road is a hennery,
Jungle fowl are flitting about in that rite
Of instinctive ritual of pecking—."

Poet: (interrupts) "We are going to a feeding.
Discomfort plagues my itching hide,
Those ants plague the fecund earth,
They are a curse concentrated in dark scurry,
Bid farewell to our brief companion—goodbye,
This memory will linger, as an aftertaste of anisette."

Milkmaid: (musing) "Annette? How did you know my name?"

A thin linen stage curtain descends as the two peripatetic figures exit right stage. In the background a rasping voice is heard above the slam of a screen door. Unintelligible rural gibberish builds up to a crescendo—there is one clear identifiable word—'breakfast'. From left stage the plaintive sonorous notes of an oboe fill the air with a nostalgic rendition of 'a blue-tail fly.'

A Gathering

"I am alone among these sticklegged chickens, as before,
Once—twice a day scrounging eggs along the henhouse
floor,
Pushing feathered fowl aside, my cackling sinecure,
Seeking eggs in every crack or splintered aperture,
They gather sheer from hunger be sunlight, wind, or rain,
Their only thought is appetite within that pellet brain."

Chorus: "Fair frisky fowl whose wattles flush with greed
Draw nigh—the crackcorn maiden scatters seed."

"We lost the leghorn rooster to a fox or hungry dog,
Chicken eating varmits filch and thieve, kill, maraud.
It's ferrets, polecats, weasels, snakes, and ringtail cats by
night,
Survival is miracle when viewed in morning light,
It's hawks and hungry osprey, twisting in a gyre,
Or careless chickenlittles straying past the chickenwire."

Chorus: "Watch now how the temptress gathers them with
corn,
Avian agitation, longevity stillborn."

"Ignore that loud Greek chorus, their tragic masks askew,
My restless flock will fill my pot, their destiny a stew.
My cyclic life revolves between the kitchen and this ground
So yellow-flecked with chickenfeed and wispy chicken
down,
Some day with changing status a profession I will choose,
Not henhouse mud but polish will you find upon my
shoes."

Chorus: "Simplistic little country lass, you seek a hallowed
grail,
Beyond reality of hens, between that dinner pail,
This was your sharing time immersed in simple toil,
The genesis of all our worth is sown, or walks the soil."

The Puzzle Woods

Here was a canopy held by oaks
So massive they would hold in thrall
A pharaoh long accustomed to great
And wondrous columns reaching upward
Into the gloom of night, or fiery day,
Yet here were colonnades of virgin forest,
Temple sites of nature where they ran
As youth, then with their children
Walking among those aisles of trees
Whose burden changed in passing seasons,
A reverent slow progression of old life
In rootlets, bough, and leaves; an arcade
With a thousand thousand crossings of limbs
Entwining their dappled nimbus onto trunks
Concealing time, direction, and our orb
In transit high above, to gleam sunburnished,
Forming lacelike filigrees on strata
Based in humid rot of leaf and stem.
All paths would veer into some maze
Inviting frowns and dark confusion
Where turns or vantage points obscured
Those dim perspectives bound to trick
The neophyte in forest depth.
Such gentle senses are not keen
When deep immersed in stands of forest,
We forget too soon that grand and spacious
Heritage of woods.

Into this rustling temple was
Communion with a God
Who in His wisdom had decreed
A leafy promenade.
Among colossal trunks a pretense one could feel,
At any turn an awesome mystic power was revealed.

That marvel, peace, was known at once,
Pervading every mind,
Too oft inflamed ambitious passions
Burdened most mankind.
Unimportant they became in that parklike solitude,
The puzzle woods, in reverie an ancient interlude.

What silver echoes graced those crowns
High in each season's winds?
Those selfsame arias were sung
To forest Amerinds.
They read those faintly trodden paths as well we scan this
text,
They solved in simple rhythms questions we perceive
complex.

They took but what was needed
Ever grateful to survive,
They too were forest creatures,
And no further need they strive
To alter what was given or destroy the joy of birth
That sheened leaves wet with droplets, or fragrant earth.

When lightning scarred the titans,
And the drumrolls crashed from high,
On the shore of darkness drifting
Came the shaman's piercing cry,
Then the puzzle woods in turmoil knew the anxious voice of man,
Clinging to their brief existence in the shelter of a clan.

There was an Indian summer,
One last time they stalked the deer,
Their forest stood abreast
Of a nameless, strange frontier,
They heard the sound of axes, but not the shaman's prayer,
As one would snuff a taper they were not, they were not there.

How were these acres spared?
Why weren't they cleared in turn?
So the puzzle woods remained
While most around were burned.
Into our lifetime it confounded sorely with its maze,
How many walks or picnics, how many holidays?

Seek here within this remnant lithograph
Some semblance of its covenant with all
Who dared this temple concourse to explore,
Adrift within the forest's shadowed pall.
Could we but dare to leave such treasures whole?
What value can one place upon a stroll?

Remnants of the Puzzle Woods

There were red cotton fields, where stood
In other years the puzzle woods,
Not even that remains, a leached and barren strand
That runs in wretched rivulets and gullies in the sand,
Brought down by mud-clogged waters in the river's turbid flow,
Watched only by this remnant oak and mistletoe.
One a giant, the other, parasite,
Alone through barren days and restless night.

What worth those forest glades and graceful fern?
The trees were bulldozed, stacked, and slowly burned.

We are a patchwork quilt, we are,
This fabric stitched in crazy patterns,
So intertwined with woe and triumph,
Folded, tossed, or spread full wide
As any timbered stand, to warm and shelter
Before death, by degrees scarcely noticed
Becomes the fate of things without momentum.
Sing of purple mountains and golden shores,
But at this moment consider what once was.

Into this void the constant winds without a shred
Of mercy, desiccated land that drew from moldy
Foliates its nourishment; where is that distant voice?
The shaman's prayer fades, a reedy cry raised
Pivot point to the abode of some greater power.

We are strong in our arrogance,
We subdued and prospered, but at cost.
The lessons came hard, they did.
The artist knows, as do so many
Some remnants should return, they should.
Generations hence could grow again, their puzzle woods.
Yet some would argue, 'what price a stroll?'
They would.

Cedar Choppers

In all things there is a winding down, the sunset
Blazing one farewell,
Where lights of soft pastel,
Glow through a darkening forest to beget,
Deepest shades of night we soon forget.

See here a hardness in their lives, tough speech,
And tougher fare,
Primitive the stare,
A place where woman, child and man will reach
Across a roughboard table as roughened hands beseech
Some shadow deity lifting dull despair.

Here the silence of unknowing wrests them free,
They seem unfettered, boisterous, crude,
Yet shackled to a woody servitude,
Trapped in a labyrinth of thickstand second growth,
Cursing aromatic toughness, oath on oath,
Unending struggles 'neath that Texas canopy,
Pitting cedar chopper 'gainst the juniper tree.

Knotty, twisted, gnarled eternal post,
Weathered gray and stapled tight with wire,
Singed by fire,
Rubbed by rutting bulls, reused, then burned,
Country staves that fence the country berm,
Stacked ever higher, higher,
Rick on drying rick seeking buyer,
Waiting out the season ringed by conifer and fern.

There are few songs, no operettas, soft etudes,
Their sharpened axe is art enough, their interludes
Sojourns to the strangers' town nearby,
Their chapel—the open sky,
Their glory—a rainbow glimpsed on high,
Their wonderment—a baby's cry,
Their chariot—a belching aged steed weighed down
To flatten leafsprings parallel to ground.

Dense is that thicket set in forest glim,
A gloomy universe of needle sighs,
Aloof from those whose calling is to hew
Unyielding fiber, oak to yew,
Whose toughness even their sharp blades defies,
Rasped by roaring chains, limb on limb.

Bare their table, bare the cots within,
Uprooted migrant clans whose tough hands seize
Whatever brief encounter with that muse
Residing in the cedar's amber ooze,
Would in their coarseness other nymphs displease,
Dryads couched in somber cypress fen.

No symbiotic myths are theirs to share,
When pressed by need ill-clad in rough attire,
Horizons stretched no further than the dish,
Reality is knowing few can wish,
Rewards are scarce suppressing all desire,
Their milieu, a numbing front, or summer's glare.

Their jostled children clutch the lorry seat,
Inured to simple fare and simpler speech,
Defining some small niche within each glade,
Where darting into daylight or the shade,
They drag obstructing debris out of reach,
Returning oft again on nimble feet.

More harshly fate has yoked some vestal bride,
Turned over by the preacher's hand to one
Expecting much where less is scarcely more
Than crude enclosures or a flapping door,
Admitting vernal gusts or broiling sun
Billowing choking dust end to side.

Woodsmen find solace in their favored kind, where music fills,
A rare encampment tossed upon this page, set down in art
For us to full imagine all the range of those who live posthaste,
Slashing passive monarchs or their stunted kin apart,
Yielding aromatic posts that shed their brown
Pervading sterile carpet muffling saw and cry
When with a crackling lurch some denizen of thickets
Long forgotten, admits the breeze and azure sky.
These are withdrawn habits none ascribe
More talents than the cording stacks or ricks
Afford as proof their essence gleans and strips
The forest bounty, heartwood, dust, and sticks.

They mulch the forest floor with burdened loads,
Patois speech in sparse abodes,
They seek no titles, fame or fortune here,
Just victuals, privacy, and store-bought beer.

Texas Horned Lizard

"I know it's hot, you took a chance,
Running at high noon in a dance
I call 'the lizard walk', skip, hop hop scratch,
Your skin a prickly pear, your face mismatched,
Ancient reptile, lord of ants and flies,
Living fossil under Texas skies,
You were there in lands not yet adrift,
Below the capricorn, beside some rift,
The artist on his belly seeks to spy
Upon you, judging thorny outline and beady eye,
Perky bright expression ne'er to change
When eons grind to dust some snow-capped range,
Your tough and dauntless lineage will survive,
Long after passing of our brief archive,
What pace change when time is stretched to this?
We speak of ages, metamorphosis,
You are a remnant darting through the sage,
A primal player from another age,
For neither greeting nor a fond 'adieu'
Would have a meaning for the likes of you,
Perhaps we are too complex for our good,
Could be that we, not you, misunderstood?
Misunderstood our niche upon this sphere,
It is us, not you, horned toad, the world must fear."

Mystical Beast

Some creatures are drawn into being,
Themselves a titanic life force,
A magnificence implanted square upon
That openness that once was, was to be
Forever, until change hung as millstones
Upon their migratory existence,
They were brute reminders of abundance
Formed in fluctuating masses on the prairie,
They lived, without a depth of knowing,
Without perception of why, why they were
The mystical beasts.

Within a nebulous awesome power of creation
Dark forms, shoulder to flank swept in unison
Upon a restless landscape of grasses, furry bison,
Whole leagues of thundering beasts bore down
In seething herds following some ancient summons,
Instincts dimly perceived but all pervading,
Turning again in tidal cycles of monumental size,
By sheer immensity declared, masters of the plains.

Even forceful masters bend,
First man was afoot,
Their fluted points were thrust
With chance effect on stragglers,
Or kicking victims of fire or fall,
Man was the gnat nipping at their hooves,
Man was a small wanderer,
Man sought in desperation sustenance
From their great strength,
Man joined their mythic being.

Man thought and thought,
Fletched the arrow, strung the bow,
Blew on his fire, and harried the herds.
But they were a universe of plenty,
And man an inconstant prairie vapor.

Unwittingly the beasts ne'er realized
When puny man climbed on the Spanish mustang,
His newfound mystical beast,
An era opened upon the Llano Estacado,
Where starving clans once fired the brush,
Now travois tracks crossed and recrossed
Wallows, streams, canyons, thickets,
Changes struck new chords, new harmonies,
Yet a finite balance swung between those horns,
And clusters of lodgepoles.

They were enshrined, the mystical beasts,
Enshrined in the needs of the centaurs,
Enshrined in legend, in their heart of hearts,
They were great medicine.
Upon them, out where only sky divided days,
All needs were met upon the stage of death.
In dying birth was engendered; in birth death was stayed,
That commissary of the plains formed herds
Of snorting pleistocene survivors,
And from their flesh
A culture came into its own.

In a whirlwind of change the warriors flew
Clutching the honda, legs braced on ribs,
Ponies paced their prey,
Tribes paced the seasons,
Antagonists fought for space
Upon a firmament ne'er twice the same,
Names of these roll from tongues once heard
As fleshed out redmen whose existence
Was the reality of mythical beasts.

Yet some few linger on the bitter edge
Of distant reservations set aside
From busy pathways crossing ancient trails,
From foothills to where old streams divide,
Their beasts still cling to life within preserves,
Their mounts foal in some corner most ignore,
Scattered flints and midden rocks remain,
And celluloid folklore.

Hordes of buffalo and hordes of men
Whose destinies were crosswise will repeat
A litany of conquest writ in blood,
Crumpling mortally maimed in cold defeat,
Pierced by hails of lead, yet dumbly struck,
A twinkling, their demise occurred like that!
A change so wrenching we can scarce comment,
That dreadful loss of prairie habitat.

The gift of mounts evolved with counting coup,
One touch for centuries, then a thrust of cultures,
Like any final wound the plains bled down,
An abyss loomed between the new and old,
A chasm of philosophy and intent tore at the peoples,
Brutalized the conflict, and left mercy an orphan.
Thus within a decade, stumbling through the smoke
Of Sharps and Creedmores, the stubborn masters of the
plains
Rotted upon the earth they had so long ruled.

Curly mesquite grasses witness still
A land now altered in the course of gain,
Roots torn out of loam borne on the winds
Await that final sculptor, rain.
It carves ravines upon a naked soil,
Fenced off where ranges once in harmony
Fed more than man could see or even count,
God's bounty coursing on an inland sea.

What is, and was could not share time or space,
Thus to extinction progress will efface.

I've read 'whose ox was agored?', 'those savages and beasts',
'They stomped the tracks', 'they tore the fences down',
'They warred on us', 'they lifted scalp tufts', 'drank
Fishberry whiskey', 'left the victims bound—'
Would one expect less when lives in ruin
Destroy free nomads mounted for the chase?
Their culture did not fade or change its stripe,
It was replaced.

Nature through upheavals has decreed,
Some survive, but many fall extinct,
Those in turn depart or change their lot,
And myriads will hover on the brink.
In rapid sequence we have pressed our hands
Against the play of forces long entwined
Upon this continent where all was shared,
And well defined.

The consequences form a spectral cloud
That trails our history like a prairie fire,
From out that blackened stubble roots will sprout,
Replacing each empire.
We hoist the image flapping on some sail,
We reproduce the symbols mute and worn,
Change apocalyptic is the fate
Of those unborn.

Remnants of Change

Old survivor, staring back at us,
Tough and pliant, fitful history,
Growing strong on wildness never dulled
By mystery.
Reflect upon your errant interlude,
Immersed in harsher rhythms, storm, or drought,
Tenacious, grave, horns wideset to survive,
Besieged without.

Turned into the frore of blizzards,
Smelling moisture far beneath dry sands,
Ringing stumbling calves with chill intent,
Or final stands.
Muzzles lowered at graybacks, or man,
Werewolves, or wolves, what mattered that?
One for hunger, one for profit slew,
Remnants altered by man's harsh fiat.

Your bones intestate linked with drastic change
Littered trampled pathways drovers carved,
Replacing bison swept from distant hills,
And mankind starved.
Pressed forever onward to board pens,
Then packed within some snaking, roaring train
Leaving tawdry outposts for the east,
To join the slain.

Slain when there no longer stretched the seas
Of rippling grasses, wave on tossing waves.
In mournful silence scarce a handful crouched
In chance enclaves.

Ancient auroch, brindled, steadfast in that gaze
Evolved by brutish energies, seasoned, tried, and raw,
Loyal, lean, and steeped in treachery,
And nature's law.
You teach us more than we instruct your kin,
You are reality, whereas we dream,
Remington conveyed that message of your kind
In lightning's gleam.
Bolting in that crashing flare of night,
As pealing thunder spooked the frantic herd,
You followed dictates primitive and sure
As ours are blurred.

Now it is us who make the reality,
We form stampedes by brilliant shafts of light
Of our own making, forces charged with fire,
Unending fright.
We have turned the peaceful evening sky
Into a junkyard filled with migrant steel,
Not flocks of trumpeting fowl,
God's weal.

Beyond whatever hills or dusty flats
You once held fief by dint of massive horns
And thrashing hooves, some part of us now gone
Our world mourns.

Buffeted all about, eclipsed in haunts so vastly dim
Where a steady chain of procreation replaced the weak,
Nourished on thorn and grasses culled among the brush,
Bloodied in the snarling desperation of the chase,
Skittish and patient as are all wild creatures fleeing
Wide eyed, clopping hoofbeats, hunter and the hunted,
Yet this old mossback ruminating there,
Could never change.

An essay on Ancel E. Nunn's folio

Our Texas is a leather hide
Stretched across an austere and generous land,
It is a challenge for those striving,
And a paradox of variety and change.
It is a throbbing tympanum of history
Reverberating on this searing anvil
Where conquerors and the conquered
Are annealed into a composite whole,
Remaining in our collective memories
As remnants of change.

There is an audacity in this land,
Steeped in this harsh, unkind environment
A panorama of ferment trickles down through time,
Time, in its transit, like some sightless bard
Ticks off each footfall, seeking some narrow
Constricted waist where eager grains
Jostle in their single flow to the underside
Of what has occurred.

Each page becomes the artist's statement,
A part of the natural order of life,
Impressed for us to envision, again,
Change—welcome and feared,
Change—persistent or perverse,
Change, leaving in its wake
Remnants of this exuberant, astringent,
Immense terrain heaved into being,
Strung along its living frontiers
Evoke profound surges of emotion,
These are precious remnants of Texas
Our Texas, remembered, engraved in a folio
Here, between the hides.

Behold, the land, outstretched before
A name was given, or features mapped;
It roils in motion between fractious winds,
It convolutes its wizened hills,
It silts within the confluence of rivers;
Life at its inception sprang from aquifers,
Nourishing successions of plants.
Foliage and grasses invited centaurs
To explore in freedom its wide domain
From brushy thickets to cypress-lined banks.

So brief their youth, the centaurs,
So harsh their pathways, they drew
On ancient lineage and their myths,
They leaped new cataracts,
They crossed strange crests,
Camped on ledges, stood alone
Within that tempestuous steppe,
Awaiting some change, as all wide spaces
Transfigure their history ever mobile,
Never at ease, anticipating with each season
That clash of cultures to come,
Within this vibrant continent
There would be attrition, and human change.

This is our Texas forever, our glory,
An amalgam of stone and old splintered boards,
Thorny limbs, flapping sheets,
Shores and canyons, glass and chrome,
Derricks whose skeletal limbs
Straddle wildcat dreams,
As round green buttons of the Ogallala
Pump fragile life into dry landscapes.
Raised in the shadows of drought,
Dreamscapes evolve, dry or fecund,
Burning a'plenty, all about.

Scattered in the orderly confusion of nature
There is a continuum of birth,
Here we capture the essence of our being,
Challenges are the norm, and peace an orphan.
It is a milieu of aggravation,
This is the product of wills,
Here the possessed and dispossessed
Know their bounds, within a disruptive
Crosscurrent of humanity; behold
The enfeebled, boisterous, heroic, magnificent,
Sinful, striving, enigmatic, restless humans
That became Texas, bled Texas, shook Texas,
Until each layer of cambium strengthened those limbs,
Like some ancient bristlecone it stands
Sturdy, erratic, and rooted to the soil.

Marred by abrasions of conflict,
Oft tattered our fabric so drear,
Riven, discarded, and frenzied with hope,
Pressured and quaking with fear,
A tapestry woven upon the expanse
Evolved in sequences of life,
Remnants will cling to the patterns o'erdrawn
Reflecting our love and our strife.

This, the exuberant immodest stark land,
Where boundaries seethe in the process of birth,
And death scythes the innocent caught where the storm
Anoints the unholy and scourges our earth,
Where soil burns dark gray 'neath a pitiless sky,
Where upwelling dust and debris
Unleashes a hell full forsaken, alone,
Inured to its dark agony.

I glory in space encompassed by unyielding winds,
Cerulean limits yet boundless, in turbulent motion,
Of seeing the infinite stretch of soil where I tread,
Deprived of restraints that cease in the depths of an ocean.

My vision still seeks through the haze for an unfettered
  view,
Dim lit in a twilight of forms that scurry pell mell
Through the brackens and lichens of time whose infinite
  fen
Is to some ages life, yet in bondage to fate, naked hell.

Horizons that undulate, choppy, plicated, and creased,
Enfolded, so rugate their surfaces toss all about
In a shambles—terrains in subduction descend to their
  source
To outline their rafts in ripples of volcanic grout.

Windblasted heights are thrust past rivers of air,
Depleting cool moisture, the lifesparing droplets of dew,
Thus leeward some desert lies thirsty, parched in its core,
Arroyos cut deep in a tableau of land's residue.

Each league is a change where the norm is perverted and
  sere,
The sparse woody twig evolves a passion to grow,
Its progeny seeds into an uneasy earth
Awaiting the bounty of clouds on the flora below.

Scarce has our soil been shifted when what but the rasp
Of nature abrades that weather hewn shard of a ledge,
Incising some rift dividing escarpments so high
Supporting with clouds tracts seamed by some errant dark
hedge.

Propelled through flumes or racing canyon foam,
Treasured debris speeds onward to finally rest
Upon some lost basin where crystalline springs will seep
Or plummet headlong from craggy alpine crests.

We glory to sense infinity spun round as webs,
Gossamer strands stretched taut through arcades of hills,
Dark loggias vaulting each sinuous trace of some path,
Beneath the cardfleece of moisture drawn outward in rills.

Within some broodcave or hollow greengourd of life,
Some glen where breezes rumple meshworks of vines,
Where fine wispy grasses disguise the seepage of flats,
Beneath the murmuring needles of tall restless pines.

Windsongs emote each drama, each epoch we know.
Our vision aspires, but our steps are fastened below.

It is the artist who preserves,
Retains for us our collective memories,
Our recollections, our mythic being,
Our legends, our facts, and fantasies,
There is perspective in art,
And the gift of perspective involves
This understanding of watersheds,
And mundane, personal moments.
It is the visual sharing of joy, and tragedy,
Shared once, and shared again,
Through the tangled weave of living,
Moments we recall upon these leaves,
Remnants of change.

Epitaph

Send for me a scribe,
That all be writ,
Debits paid with balanced books,
Farewells penned and agony relived—
Yet one more boon, take this,
A purse to one who fleshes out
Our past—the artist.
Without a drawing of these things
We would not know,
From whence we came, or why.

SCW

About the Author

SAMUEL CARMON WOOLVIN is a pathologist residing in Corpus Christi. Long a personal friend of the artist and a transplanted Texan since 1967 he has been active studying the history of the region, restoring a national registry historical site in the hill country, and continuing a lifelong hobby of writing and collecting art. His friendship with Ancel and Reneta, through all the periods of the artist's development, grew into a unique opportunity to write serious descriptions of his works, Remnants of Change being one group of several still being compiled.

His wife, Alma, is a descendent of several of the oldest families in Texas. Having a close association with the Hispanic as well as the Anglo-German communities in Texas has given the author an opportunity to understand and relate to many Texans and their forebears. Out of the amalgam of a regional past he has collected an extensive library to draw from when writing. Some years ago he gave a number of works of art to U.T., Houston Museum of Fine Arts, and several churches. Among these was a large major painting by Ancel Nunn, now in the Humanities Research Center in Austin. Through the medium of poetry he brings into focus the works of an artist of stature, Ancel E. Nunn.

About the Artist

ANCEL E. NUNN, born in Baylor County, Texas, has received a number of awards, including the Texas Arts Alliance Award and the Chicago '76 Certificate of Excellence. His work has been widely exhibited and has appeared in numerous publications. It has been featured in two films produced for television, one for the Public Broadcasting System by the Institute of Texan Cultures. His paintings are represented in many Texas museums and private collections. The artist's early studies (1940s) in the Dallas–Ft. Worth area brought him in contact with many of the Texas Regionalists and his philosophy of art reflects this period of time. Mr. Nunn's studio is in Palestine, Texas.

REMNANTS of CHANGE

has been set in Berkeley Old Style type
by G&S Typesetters, Austin.
Printed on Mohawk Superfine by Best Printing, Inc., Austin
Bound by Custom Bookbinders, Austin
Designed and Produced by
Whitehead & Whitehead, Smithville
1991